LAND OF FUN

The Story of an Old-Fashioned Amusement Park for the Ages

Chris Lindsley

For information about the book, contact:
Chris Lindsley
408 Circle Avenue
Takoma Park, MD 20912
clindsley@starpower.net

ISBN 978-0-578-46825-9

First Edition, 2019

Printed in the United States of America

Designed by Michelle Bamburak

Visit the book website at www.Land-of-Fun.com

For Deborah, Graham, Olivia and mom and dad.

PHOTO CREDITS

TABLE OF CONTENTS

INTRODUCTION:
My Funland Story

When I was 4 in the summer of 1968, a family friend was unable to use the beach house she had booked in Rehoboth Beach, Delaware, and asked my parents if they wanted it. That chance offer started a 50-year family tradition of vacationing in Rehoboth Beach each summer for a week that always included visits to Funland.

I went from wild-eyed kid on the rides, to begging my parents for quarters so I could play pinball in the arcade as a preteen, to working there for six summers in high school and college, to being the parent of two kids who love Funland. I experienced the park through their eyes in a whole new way.

Funland, and the four generations of the Fasnacht family who have owned and operated the amusement park since 1962, have had such a huge influence on my life that I was inspired to write this book to share what makes them so special.

I am not an unbiased observer; I started this project as a big Funland and Fasnacht family fan. After almost two years of interviewing well over 100 people – Funland customers, former employees, town officials and business owners, people in the amusement park industry and more – I'm even more of a believer today. There are important lessons and advice here for people of all ages. To me, it's a story of a family that puts people and community before profits. It also shows what can be accomplished when you share a common goal – to provide customers with the kind of experience, value and enter-tainment you'd like to receive – without worrying about who gets the credit.

As family patriarch Al Fasnacht says, "One of the greatest things in life is the opportunity to do something for someone else." He and his family have done just that at Funland since 1962, and have taken many others, like me, along for the ride. I could not be more grateful.

Chris Lindsley
Takoma Park, Maryland
April 2019

CHAPTER 1:

The Origins of Funland

"Did I know Funland would be such a success?
No, but I thought if we worked hard, provided a good value,
treated our customers well and enjoyed making others
happy that we had a chance."
– Al Fasnacht

Sport Center in 1957. The Fasnacht family purchased it in 1962 and renamed it Funland.

At a quaint summer beach destination in Delaware, dubbed the "Nation's Summer Capital" for all the Washingtonians who vacation there, lives a small, family-owned amusement park that has called Rehoboth Beach home since 1962. This is not just any amusement park; its owners place a premium on offering affordable family fun for all ages. In a beach resort known for multiple generations of families gathering for summer vacation every year, this park with a most appropriate name – Funland – is a throwback to an earlier time when these sort of parks were a gathering place for many and where people went to have a good time. Add to the mix that Funland has five rides it has operated since John F. Kennedy was president, that customers routinely comment on how safe they feel and the family memories and sense of nostalgia the park creates, and you have a place a former Rehoboth mayor calls "indispensable" for the niche it provides for families with young kids.

Funland has 20 rides, including a unique Haunted Mansion attraction the family built from scratch that is considered by some experts as one of the best in the country; 17 midway/carnival/amusement games such as the

Derby (a horse racing game), Whac-a-Mole and 12 Skee-Ball lanes; and an arcade. All this on one acre of prime, beachfront real estate, just a few hundred yards south of the town's center and showy, ever-changing and eponymous promenade, Rehoboth Avenue.

There is something about families and summer vacation destinations; it's as though we are all searching for that special place, and once we find it, we are unwilling to go anywhere else. After all, there's a lot at stake for the entire family in leaving a sure thing for someplace new, no matter how highly recommended.

"In Rehoboth, we take a lot of pride in the intergenerational experience," said Sam Cooper, who was Rehoboth's mayor from 1990 to 2017. "We have a lot of people here who were the grandkids of people that vacationed here 50 years ago, so I think there is a special meaning in taking your grandchild when he is 3 years old and having him ride the Boats that you remember from 50 years ago."

◆ ◆ ◆ ◆

My family's first Rehoboth Beach vacation, in the summer of 1968, was happenstance as much as anything. That we have returned for a week every summer since is anything but, as it has become like a second hometown.

Happenstance is also a good word to describe the origins of Funland. The Fasnacht family of Hershey, Pennsylvania, owned a small, picnic amusement park that operated mostly on summer weekends called Willow Mill Park in nearby Mechanicsburg – about halfway between Harrisburg and Carlisle. Al, known as Big Al, and Esther Fasnacht, known as Sis – "because she had several brothers, and that's what they called her, and everyone else did the same" – purchased Willow Mill in 1956. Sons Al and Don, then in their mid to late 20s, played major roles at the park: Don and Big Al handled the mechanical work, while Al supervised the personnel and the grounds, and Sis managed the office. The entire family combined forces and often recruited others to prepare and serve barbecue chicken dinners – with baked beans, potato chips, apple sauce and a drink – for groups as large as 1,000 people at a cost of $1.50 per person.

"Every once in a while they would call us and say, 'Do you have any time to come and help us with our chicken dinner?'" remembers Nancy Zimmerman. She, along with her husband, Dick, who went on to become the CEO of Hershey Foods, were longtime friends of Al and his wife, Jean. "We always said 'Yes,' and our daughters loved to ride the rides while Dick and I were working on the chicken barbecue. Those were fun times."

Memories of Willow Mill Park, which the Fasnacht family owned from 1956 to 1967.

When not eating, Willow Mill's patrons were riding a wooden roller coaster, bumper cars, a carousel, Whip, Sky Fighter, miniature train and a Chris-Craft speedboat on the Conodoguinet Creek that bordered the park. The park also had an arcade, concessions, games, food stands and, most importantly, 10 pavilions for group outings, which could accommodate as many as 2,000.

Amusement park owners are always looking for the next ride, game or attraction to create some buzz, and the Fasnachts were no different. In 1961, the family vacationed for a few days just south of Rehoboth Beach near Indian River Inlet. One night they went to Sport Center, an amusement park on the Rehoboth Beach boardwalk that opened in 1939, and featured kiddie rides, bumper cars, a batting cage, a miniature golf course, Skee-Ball lanes, pinball machines and a Spill-the-Milk game. They saw a ride called the Helicopters that was one of the first for kids in which the rider controlled the vehicle's movement.

After watching the Helicopters, Al went to find Sport Center's owner, Anthony (Jack) Dentino, to express his interest in some day purchasing one for Willow Mill Park. Dentino had his own agenda for the conversation, and quickly asked Al if he had any interest in buying Sport Center. Al relayed this conversation to his father, but both had little interest initially. After sleeping on it, however, they decided to return to Sport Center that night and get more information on the park from Dentino.

◆ ◆ ◆ ◆

Negotiations began in the fall of 1961, and by December they reached an agreement: The Fasnachts would buy Sport Center for $175,000. This included a combined 7½ lots on Surf Avenue, Delaware Avenue and Brooklyn Avenue. The settlement date was set for March 15, 1962. On March 6-8, the Great Atlantic Storm, also called the Ash Wednesday Storm, a devastating Nor'easter, battered the Mid-Atlantic coast for five high tides. The powerful tides destroyed almost all of Rehoboth's boardwalk, and every structure fronting the boardwalk except one was either washed out to sea or so severely damaged they had to be demolished. The exception was Sport Center's original structure at the corner of Delaware Avenue. Its doors and floor were gone, and the two-story building sank 19 inches, but it was salvageable. A much larger 50-foot by 75-foot section of Sport Center was washed away, and some of the Bumper Cars were transported to the beach and so buried in sand that only the top part of the trolley poles were visible.

Dentino contacted the Fasnachts and suggested they meet in Rehoboth to examine the damage. He also offered to refund the Fasnachts' deposit and allow them to get out of the deal during the same phone call. The Fasnachts, though, were still interested in moving forward, depending on the size of the damage allowance they could negotiate. Since the storm damage was caused by water, the insurance companies Dentino had policies with on Sport Center were not liable because the extended coverage expressly excluded losses from water damage.

Al picks up the story from there: "Mr. Dentino said he asked an insurance appraiser to give him an estimate of the damage, and together they came up with $25,000. I told him I had no experience in any kind of appraisal work, but that it looked like significantly more loss. I promised him our family would discuss it on our trip back home to Hershey and would give him an answer in the morning. As we were backing out of the driveway, I saw Mr. Dentino run into the house – I believe to consult with his wife – and as we started pulling away, he came out the door waving for us to stop. He said they decided to increase the damage allowance to $50,000, at which point we had a deal."

Al said the threat of future storms did little to sway him and his family from what they thought was a good opportunity at the right time.

"It was unlikely the city of Rehoboth Beach would not rebuild the boardwalk, and we felt as long as the city wanted to stay in the resort business, we should have a chance to succeed," Al said. "We realized we were limited with how far we could go with Willow Mill Park, so we decided to branch out and see what we could do at the beach. I also distinctly recall old timers saying that killer storms like this happen once every 50 years. That didn't mean it couldn't happen again in the next 10 minutes, but we realized history was on our side there."

The Great Atlantic Storm of 1962 left Funland's Merry-Go-Round exposed to the salt air from the ocean.

Amazingly, Rehoboth rebuilt the boardwalk before the summer tourist season, and Funland, as the Fasnacht-owned park came to be called – "I came up with the name," Al said. "I thought Funland described the park we wanted to create much better than Sport Center" – was open for business just months after the massive storm. The Fasnacht family, never ones to shy away from physical labor, went to work, cleaning up the storm debris, jacking up the storm-surviving structure almost two feet and building a floor using boardwalk wood salvaged from the storm so it matched the level of the new boardwalk, and Funland was ready, at least in a manner of speaking. There wasn't enough time, or money, to replace the large section of the Sport Center building that was washed out to sea – which would be rebuilt after the summer season ended – so that left the Merry-Go-Round exposed to the salt air on the east or ocean side that first summer. That was one of 12 rides in 1962, and one of five – the Boats, Fire Engines, Sky Fighters and Helicopters being the others – still in operation today.

		Funland Ride History		
Year First Appeared at Funland#	Ride	Year First Appeared at Funland#	Ride
1962	Bumper Cars	1981	Bumper Cars
1962	Fire Engines*	1982	Paratrooper*
1962	Helicopters*	1983	Wagon Wheeler
1962	Kiddie Merry-Go-Round	1984	Kiddie Swing*
1962	Merry-Go-Round*	1984	Gravitron*
1962	Miniature Train	1988	Bumper Cars
1962	Pinwheel	1988	Mini Himalaya*
1962	Sky Fighters*	1989	Jeep Ride
1962	Turnpike	1989	Jungle of Fun
1962	Wet Boats*	1990	Sea Dragon*
1962	Kiddie Whip	1996	Jungle of Fun
1962	Tubs-O-Fun	1998	Chaos
1963	Bumper Cars	1999	Frog Hopper
1964	Crazy Dazy*	2000	Trucks*
1965	Flying Cages	2001	Bumper Cars*
1971	Motorcycles*	2004	Free Fall*
1972	18 Skooters	2005	Kiddie Ferris Wheel*
1974	Paratrooper	2008	SuperFlip
1975	Moonwalk	2014	SimRider*
1977	Trabant	2017	SuperFlip 360*
1979	Haunted Mansion*	2018	Jungle of Fun*

#Note: Many rides in operation during Funland's first summer in 1962 were a part of Sport Center, which was located on the same site from 1939 to 1961.
*Rides at Funland in the Summer of 2019.

Business was very slow in the summer of 1962, as word had gotten out that Rehoboth, and other Atlantic Coast beach towns, were disaster areas. "I think we make more money on a busy day today than we did all of that first summer," Al said. That year, Funland employed 13 boys, who were paid $15 a week. Ticket prices debuted at one ticket for 10 cents and 12 for $1. Little did anyone know at the time, but ticket prices would remain unchanged for 25 years. Rehoboth had a new business that would help shape the town's family-friendly reputation for the next half century and beyond.

MY FUNLAND STORY: Laurie Strongin, CEO, Hope for Henry Foundation

Laurie Strongin is the CEO of the Hope for Henry Foundation, whose mission is to reinvent how hospitals care for seriously ill children through innovative programs. The foundation is named for her son, Henry, who died of Fanconi anemia — a rare, inherited blood disorder that leads to bone marrow failure — at the age of 7. Strongin wrote a book about Henry's life called Saving Henry: A Mother's Journey. In the book, she talked about how Funland was one of Henry's favorite places. Strongin was very familiar with Funland: her parents had taken her on its rides when she was a kid. She couldn't wait to share that experience with her kids and said she "always" keeps a green Funland ticket in her wallet, which serves as a good luck charm.

Whenever we had a chance, we would take our kids to Rehoboth Beach. And for Henry before his bone marrow transplant, he had no idea he was sick, and so many of his memories from his very youngest years were spent running around the beach and having a great time, and, of course, going to Funland.

Laurie Strongin and her son, Henry, on the Paratrooper. Laurie started the Hope for Henry Foundation in his memory.

Every summer there was a different favorite ride, and Henry and his younger brother, Jack, loved playing the games. Henry was really good at the basketball shooting game, and he would always come home with arms filled with stuffed animals.

We made a trip to Funland right before we were to leave for Minneapolis, Minnesota, for Henry's bone marrow transplant. As I said in my book, when Henry was born, one of the things I most looked forward to was taking him to Funland and riding on the Paratrooper together. On this visit, he asked if he could ride on it with me; I wished that ride would have gone on forever. Henry was one of those kids who always had a grin on his face and a sparkle in his eye, and I experienced both during that ride.

Funland is such a special place; I think it's the combination of the sounds, the smells and the sunshine — everything in life that is fun and happy. Like a Bruce Springsteen song, but for children. I have the biggest smile on my face right now just thinking about Funland.

When I am in Rehoboth Beach today, I get up early in the morning and walk to the end of the boardwalk and back. I do that by myself, and I think about Henry. He died on December 11, 2002, and it doesn't seem that long ago. I love being at the beach and walking to Funland and just thinking about him and all these incredibly fun memories. My husband and I go every summer, and we play Skee-Ball and I feel like part of him is still there. His spirit lives on there. It's like I can hear his laughter when I am there. It is a beautiful thing.

CHAPTER 2:

All in the Family –
Four Generations and Counting

*"It takes a special kind of commitment to keep a facility like Funland going.
As I like to say, they are not just businesses, they are family heirlooms.
These family operators feel an obligation to maintain that for
the next generation, and that is certainly true in Funland's case."*
– Jim Futrell, amusement park historian

Four generations of the Fasnacht family, summer of 2018.

A family trip to the Delaware shore in the summer of 1961 led to the Fasnachts buying Sport Center on the Rehoboth Beach boardwalk in the spring of 1962 and rechristening it Funland, and the rest, as they say, is history. Four generations of Fasnachts – made up of the Fasnacht, Curry, Henschke, Ginder, Darr, Hendricks and Golaszewski families – have operated Funland from the start with the help of staff hired for the summer, with a fifth generation not far behind.

So how rare is this? Consider that only about 30 percent of family businesses survive into the second generation, 12 percent into the third generation and 3 percent into the fourth generation, according to Joseph Astrachan, Ph.D., editor, Family Business Review, 2009.

"Quite often people ask me how long our family has been doing this," Al said. "When I tell them we started in 1962, they shake their head in disbelief, and often say something to the effect that 'Our family could never do that.' Hearing something like that makes you count your blessings.

"One key factor is that our time together in a business atmosphere is limited. We are here in early May, and we go home in mid to late September. So it's not like we are here bumping into each other 52 weeks a year, a benefit most other businesses do not have."

It's interesting listening to family members talk about the different generations. They are G2s or G3s or G4s. Like many family businesses, this one started small. The first generation, or G1s, were brothers Al and Don's parents, Big Al and Sis. The G2s are Al and Don, and their wives, Jean and Dolores (Dee), both of whom have passed away (Jean in 2013 and Dee in 2017). The G3s are Al and Don's kids — seven total — and their spouses, the G4s are the G3s' kids and spouses, and the G5s are the G4s' kids. Most of the G3s, G4s and G5s have spent few summers away from Funland, so it has literally become a home away from home.

◆ ◆ ◆ ◆

The third generation (G3s) remember their early summers at the beach, playing with their siblings and cousins, getting to know Rehoboth and that summer's crew of high school and college employees. They also remember gradually getting into the business, adding responsibility and hours as they got older. It is good to point out here that Rehoboth in the 1970s and 1980s wasn't nearly as popular a destination as it is today.

I remember many summer beach days in the middle of the week in the 1980s when you would have little or no activity at the ride or game you were working. After all, most people visited Rehoboth for the beach, and these lazy summer days were in sharp contrast to those nights, when it seemed like all of those beach families would descend on Funland and fill the park with noise, excitement and energy. They also created lines for some rides and games that, while not incredibly long or burdensome — except, perhaps, for the Haunted Mansion — always moved quickly and tended to be very friendly.

I was always struck by the scene of parents, who I imagined to be pretty busy and demanding in their day jobs, to be just fine with the relaxed beach vibe and being very willing to wait their turn while enjoying their surroundings. Such is the nature of Funland, which seems to bring out the best in many people.

FASNACHT FAMILY TREE

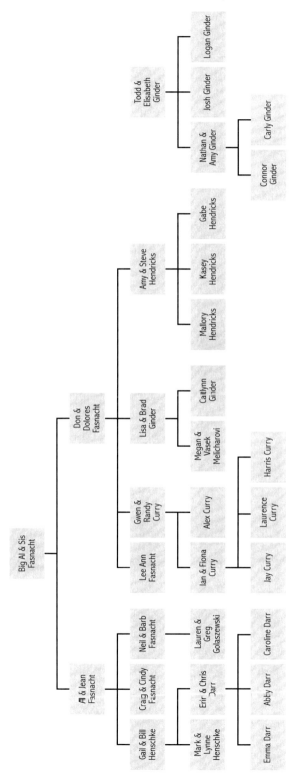

Big Al & Sis Fasnacht

- **A & Jean Fasnacht**
  - **Gail & Bill Henschke**
    - **Mark & Lynne Henschke**
      - Emma Darr
      - Abby Darr
      - Caroline Darr
  - **Craig & Cindy Fasnacht**
    - **Erin & Chris Darr**
  - **Neil & Barb Fasnacht**
    - **Lauren & Greg Golaszewski**

- **Don & Dolores Fasnacht**
  - **Lee Ann Fasnacht**
  - **Gwen & Randy Curry**
    - **Ian & Fiona Curry**
      - Jay Curry
      - Laurence Curry
      - Harris Curry
    - **Alex Curry**
  - **Lisa & Brad Ginder**
    - **Megan & Vasek Melicharovi**
    - **Caitlynn Ginder**
  - **Amy & Steve Hendricks**
    - Mallory Hendricks
    - Kasey Hendricks
    - Gabe Hendricks
  - **Todd & Elisabeth Ginder**
    - **Nathan & Amy Ginder**
      - Connor Ginder
      - Carly Ginder
    - Josh Ginder
    - Logan Ginder

"I remember one day I was working a game, and the change bag was below my knees as I was probably 8 or 9 at the time, and some older ladies were not happy that I was working because I was so little," said Don and Dee's youngest daughter, Amy. "When I would tell that to Grandma Sis, she would say, 'Just tell them you own the place.' So that's what I would do. People got a kick out of that."

Gwen, Lee Ann and Lisa Fasnacht in the early 1960s.

Amy's older sisters, Gwen, Lee Ann and Lisa, remember getting up at 10 am three to four days a week to help their mother clean and fill paint bottles for Funland's spin paint game. The way this worked was the person running the game would place a rectangular paint canvas into a holder that was down about a foot or so from the top of the spin paint platform. The customers had several paint bottles of different colors and pressed a button to make the frame spin around. They could put paint on the canvas while it was motionless or as it was spinning, and could continue pretty much until they were happy with their artwork, which was then put into a paper frame. This activity used a lot of paint, hence the need to regularly clean and fill the bottles.

"I remember our mom would yell up to us, 'It's paint morning,' and that meant we had to go down in the basement under the office and scrape paint bottles, and mom would fill them," Lee Ann said. "That was one of my first jobs. I still remember it cost 35 cents for people to create a spin painting."

Other jobs for the young Fasnacht kids included helping out in the office, stocking prizes for the games, giving breaks to the ride operators and other duties as assigned. It was nothing like what their school friends from back home in Hershey were doing for the summer.

"I enjoyed learning about the business, because you get a different perspective when you are a part of it. You also realize how much work goes into it," Lee Ann said. "I remember working in the ticket booth at a time when most kids my age were not able to get a job. They said: 'You're making money?' It was a good experience, and I always enjoyed explaining to people what my summer life was like, because they thought it was pretty neat."

Gwen said what was not so neat were cloudy days. That meant families who would normally go to the beach were often looking for other things to do, with Funland being one of their most attractive options. On those days, it was an all-hands-on-deck situation, and the younger family members quickly learned what that meant for them.

"We always dreaded the bad beach days because we were so much more crowded, and we all had to pitch in to work," Gwen said. "There were no telephones in our houses, so Uncle Allen, when he needed extra help, would come over to our house and tell us what he needed us to do. I remember one time I happened to look out the window. I saw him coming across the street, and I went out the back door. I really didn't want to work that day. For some reason that has always stuck in my mind."

♦ ♦ ♦ ♦

Al has always said all family members are welcome to join the business as long as they are willing to work hard. Al and his brother Don set the example for the generations that followed. There was little discussion about what needed to be done. They just did it, and when they finished a job they went to help others.

A part of what's commonly referred to as the Silent Generation, Al and Don basically started from scratch, where whatever success they achieved resulted from their hard work. Nothing was given to them, and born right around the Great Depression – Al in 1928 and Don in 1932 – they knew the value of a dollar and wanted to save as much money as possible. To Al, being willing to work hard has been fundamental to their remaining a family business since 1962.

"I've always felt if you are part of our family and want to work at Funland, that's fine, but be sure you understand you have to carry your share of the load," Al said. "It would be terrible if you had someone come in who said they wanted to do that but then didn't."

♦ ♦ ♦ ♦

Four generations of the Fasnacht family, summer of 1992.

One of the biggest obstacles in businesses making it to a second generation, much less a fourth, is that with new generations come new ideas. We all experience this. Think about how your parents and their parents did things, or your kids and their kids do things. The difference is, you're probably not in business with them, which adds another layer of complexity.

The Fasnacht family is no different. As the third generation nears traditional retirement age, they are starting to pass the torch to the fourth generation. To ease this transition, the family is working with the Delaware Valley Family Business Center, a consulting company that specializes in guiding multi-generational family businesses through the unique challenges they face.

"We are in the process of working through some issues, such as how our [fourth] generation succeeds and how do we take all the great and wonderful things about Funland and continue them while being willing to adapt to a change in time," said Ian Curry, the son of G3s Gwen and Randy Curry. "Delaware Valley is helping us with this. It is nice to have a neutral party where you feel safe talking about certain things and your ideas. Sometimes having a new idea can be scary: We've always done it this way, why do you want to change? The biggest thing for us at the moment is strengthening our relationships and providing us with a structure to be successful in the future. Delaware Valley's belief is if you have a strong family – what it calls building family muscle – the business will be fine.

"The biggest thing for us is strengthening our relationships with each other. We recently had an informal family picnic where everyone brought something and it was nice. It wasn't celebrating a holiday or birthday; it was just getting together as a family and socializing and having fun without talking about business."

Ian said there has been some resistance within the family to working with an outside company. The idea is not for Delaware Valley to tell the family what to do; rather, Ian said its role is to help guide the family along a path, especially as some generations step back and others take on larger roles.

Given that only about 3 percent of family-owned businesses make it to the fourth generation, and that Funland has been thriving since the early to mid 1960s, one could ask what a company like Delaware Valley can possibly tell a family like the Fasnachts. Sally Derstine, a senior family business adviser and Delaware Valley managing partner, said generational transitions are never easy, even for long-established companies.

"They are very complex because there are overlapping, exquisitely intertwined family issues, business issues, and ownership issues," Derstine said. "Each generation needs to figure out how they will transition leadership, responsibilities and roles in a way that honors the family and the business. ... Transitions involve change, and change is uncomfortable. The Fasnachts have a deep commitment to each other, to Funland and to their faith, which gives them the capacity to be open to improving practices, systems and processes that will serve their customers well. Generational transitions are a delicate dance where the leading generation needs to mentor and let go while the rising generation steps up and into new responsibilities in an aligned way, which inevitably includes adapting to change for the common good. I really commend the Fasnachts for making the choice to work on their business instead of just in the business, which is crucial for family business continuity."

◆ ◆ ◆ ◆

Much has changed during Funland's existence in terms of running a business. There are many more rules and regulations today, an increased emphasis on safety and security, and much more demand on the family, not only during the months Funland is open, due primarily to larger crowds, but during the off-season as well to keep the park and all of its games and rides in top shape and ready for another summer.

"We are down at Funland working much more during the off-season than we used to," Bill Henschke, a G3, said. "And working so closely with the same people for much of the year, you get disagreements, but they are not on a personal level, and we do a good job of working out any problems that come up. The most important thing is that we get along well and like spending time together. We all used to take an annual ski trip to Mount Snow in Vermont each winter, and we see a lot of each other when we are home in the Hershey area. We're fortunate we get to do so much with family, and that we all get along so well."

◆ ◆ ◆ ◆

Al and Don's children, the G3s, have gone from literally growing up at Funland during their summers to, in some cases, working side by side with their children now. They get to watch and interact with their grandchildren in the same family compound where they were raised. Like Funland customers who remember three and four generations of family members going on rides, the Fasnacht family is creating similar memories with its extended family in a setting that in some ways has changed very little over the last half century.

"It's wonderful to be on the porch and see the kids out there playing," Gwen Curry said. "It brings back memories of us as kids doing the exact same thing. We're very lucky to have this opportunity, and it really is enjoyable."

Every day during the season, the family takes a mid-morning break and gathers in front of the Jungle of Fun for coffee, often some baked goods and fellowship. I've attended some of these informal gatherings, called "Coffee Break," that to me are an indication of the families' tight bond. Not only do they work

Fifth-generation family members Jay Curry (left) and Emma Darr get some hands-on experience.

long hours together from May through mid-September, but most spend their off-season living within 15 miles of each other in the fall, winter and spring. Some families take vacations together, and there are other large family outings that would not happen if they did not enjoy each other's company.

"From my perspective, being able to operate a family business such as Funland and for everyone to get along and pull together is amazing," said Alan Kanter, a longtime amusement park professional and family friend. "And if I could be Al and Don for a moment, what a great thing to have all of your children, grandchildren and great-grandchildren around you all summer while you are supposedly working. You're really not working, though, because you are doing what you really want to do, and that's providing fun and making memories for people, including yourself."

Al said it is about keeping families together.

"Some of the problems in America, as I see it, revolve around the fact that our family units deteriorate," Al said. "So being a part of something that keeps the family together and gives them enjoyment is important, and we need more things that enable us to succeed with our family."

MY FUNLAND STORY:
Janette Hartney Grieb

I have been going to Funland since I was a child. My grandparents had a little place in Millsboro, Delaware [about 20 miles from Rehoboth Beach], so I spent a lot of my childhood at Funland. And then years later, when I had a daughter – Lorelei – I couldn't wait to take her to Funland. When we would go to the park and she would see Al, she assumed he was "Mr. Funland."

She and I were walking outside of Funland in March of 2016, and we saw a man cleaning. Lorelei, who was 4 at the time, wondered if it was Mr. Funland, and so she quietly went over to tell him how much she loves Funland. Al thanked her and asked if she wanted a tour. He held her hand and gave her a tour inside the park. It was the coolest day ever.

Al giving Lorelei her own personal Funland tour.

CHAPTER 3:
Brothers Partnership Key to Success

"Don and my father [Al] were the perfect team – my dad did the hiring and had the business and financial background, and Don kept stuff running. And one without the other would have brought Funland to a screeching halt."
– Neil Fasnacht

Al (left) and Don have led Funland by example.

Al and his younger brother, Don, were accomplished wrestlers at Hershey High School; both finished second in the state championships in the 138-pound weight class in different years. Their wrestling success came as no surprise to those who know them, as it speaks to their work ethic, competitiveness, determination, personal accountability and other qualities that translated well to operating an amusement park. In wrestling, it's not just about beating your opponent; you also need to manage your weight. Wrestling has 10 weight classes, and you have to "make weight" – weigh no more than, say, 138 pounds if you are wrestling in the 138-pound weight class – at the weigh-in before the match. If not, you can't wrestle at that weight.

"In wrestling, it is one on one. You can't blame anybody else if you have a shortcoming. By the same token, when you win, it is your victory. I think that aspect is important," Al said. "The other aspect is making weight. You have a responsibility, and no one is going to do that for you. You have to have the discipline to want to do it. Wrestling is the best of both worlds. You are part of a team, but it is an individual sport, and winning or losing is up to you. I think there is something about wrestling that cements friendships and loyalties more than other sports do and creates a brotherhood."

The Fasnacht brothers did not confine this philosophy to the mat. While they were growing up, their dad, Big Al, built two homes the family lived in, and during the construction of the second house, they lived with their grandparents. Al and Don would occasionally begin impromptu matches in the house, much to their grandmother's chagrin.

"We used to end up in the middle of my grandmother's living room, and she would have a fit," Don said. "She was moving furniture out on the porch and screaming at us at the same time."

◆ ◆ ◆ ◆

Al and Don developed different and, from an amusement park perspective, complementary career paths, based at least in part on following in their parents' footsteps. Their mom, Sis, worked full time for the Hershey Trust Company as a secretary for Ezra Hershey, a cousin to Milton Hershey, who founded both the Hershey Company, commonly called Hershey's, and the town of Hershey. At both Willow Mill Park and Funland, Sis was the book-keeper in the early years. Al was like-minded, as he majored in accounting at Penn State University. Their father, Big Al, worked for many years as an electrician at Hershey Estates, the company that operated all of the subsidiary companies not affiliated with the chocolate company in Hershey. He went on to work as a mechanic for Otis Elevator before handling mechanical responsibilities at both Willow Mill and Funland. Don was in a vocational electric program at Hershey High School. After gradua-tion he worked for several years with his dad at Otis before enlisting in the Air Force, where he performed electrical and mechanical maintenance during his four years of service. Upon discharge in 1956, Don cut

Al and Don's parents, Big Al and Sis, ran Funland in the early years.

meat for his father-in-law, who owned a grocery store. One winter of that was enough, though – "too much inside work for me," Don said – and he worked at Willow Mill full time in the summer of 1957.

Al took over the bookkeeping duties from his mom at Willow Mill in 1962 and at Funland in 1968. He also ran both businesses and was in charge of personnel, while Don worked closely with his dad on the mechanical side, keeping the rides running before taking on the maintenance at both parks. For the six summers the Fasnachts owned and operated both Willow Mill and Funland – from 1962 through 1967 – Al and Don ran Willow Mill and their parents ran Funland. The summer of 1968, following the sale of Willow Mill after the 1967 season, was the first time the family all worked together in Rehoboth.

One of Al's early business decisions was to set up two companies; one for the amusement park assets – Seaside Amusements, Inc. – and another one for the real estate properties they owned – both land and houses in Rehoboth – Fasnacht Realty Company, Inc. His reasoning was that this arrangement might prevent an attachment of their real estate holdings in the event of a future lawsuit related to Funland.

"Our lawyers just smiled and assured me that the idea sounded good in theory, but in practice it would not work that way," Al said. "Fortunately, we have never had to find out."

Ride safety is critical to any amusement park, and Don has been the guiding force in this area for most of Funland's existence. Amusement park rides like those at Funland require almost constant maintenance during the summer season because of the nonstop wear and tear. The presence of sand and salt air also does the equipment no favors. It is truly a 24/7 job during the season, and Don led the way by example.

"There would be an issue or problem with a ride, and Don would walk right in and in two seconds would tell you what to do to fix it. He could see it right away," said Bill Henschke, who is married to Al's daughter, Gail, and joined the business in 1977, serving a variety of roles, from ride maintenance to accounting. "Sometimes the rest of us [who perform ride maintenance] would just look at him and shake our heads, but that is the way it was. He could fix anything."

Al said Don's acumen was key to their success. "I have always said the most important contributors to our success, by far, are the mechanical people, and Don has led the effort," Al said. "Not only could Don work on anything, no matter what the problem was, and come up with a solution, but he could solve the problem with the supplies we had on hand. He never had to go a long way to find something to fix it."

◆ ◆ ◆ ◆

Don has had a lot of help keeping the rides in working order. In addition to his dad and Henschke, Randy Curry, who is married to Gwen, one of Don's four daughters, joined the business in 1979; Brad Ginder, who married Lisa, another of Don's daughters, joined the business in 1986; and one of Brad's younger brothers, Todd, who worked at Funland for more than five summers as part of the non-family crew, joined the business with his wife, Elisabeth, in 1992. They have all played key roles in making it possible to use almost solely in-house family to maintain the rides.

Most of the credit for that goes to Don, but you would never hear him say that. A soft-spoken and humble man of few words, he has been a leader, and teacher, by example. Don has been back home in Hershey in recent summers to care for his wife, Dee, who was suffering from Alzheimer's disease. Dee passed away in late February 2017. Though away from Funland, Don continues to assist, working on motors, making drive shafts for rides and machining other parts from his home shop, while also serving as a ready consultant and adviser to those on site.

Randy Curry with Don.

When facing a new or difficult problem with a ride, Curry said, "I think to myself, WWDD, or 'What Would Don Do?' I've had many situations over the last 40 years where I am pounding my head trying to find a solution, only for him to come by and say, 'Why don't you look at this?' or 'If I were you, this is what I would do.' He has such a vast knowledge of mechanical issues, has many years of hands-on experience and is seemingly always able to think things out. He is an incredible resource."

Thinking is something Don did a lot of, as there always seemed to be problems meriting his attention. He did his best thinking on his porch at night after work, often solving issues that had vexed him earlier in the day. Safety was always the top priority, and while Funland's record in that area has been very good, the ever-present possibility that something could go wrong was never far from his mind.

"Growing up, if I didn't do something right, my mother would make me do it until it was right. That was a good lesson for me as far as ride mainte- nance, as people could get hurt if things weren't done correctly," Don said. "The responsibility on my shoulders to make sure everything was done right and safe at Funland was pretty tough at times. I had a lot of years where by the end of the summer, I was pretty washed out."

◆ ◆ ◆ ◆

Al had a sense after graduating from Hershey High School that he wanted to study accounting in college. He spent the next two years at Hershey Junior College, which Milton Hershey established and made available free of charge to anyone who lived in Derry Township, of which Hershey is a part, or to any family member of a Hershey employee. Little did he know at the time just how much motivation he would have to excel in his first accounting class.

"I had a professor in accounting who was not sharp," Al said. "He had the answer book for our practice sets, and he would keep it in his drawer. When someone would ask a question, he'd slide that door open, look down and give an answer. It got to the point where the kids, my fellow students, thought I was doing the teaching. They would ask a question, and then the professor would say, 'Mr. Fasnacht, what do you think about that?' and I would give what I thought was the answer. It would get so bad at times I wasn't sure I was even in the ballpark, but I would give something because I knew he wasn't going to.

"In retrospect, maybe that caused me to work harder, so that when he would call on me, I would have an idea of what was going on."

Al spent his final two years of college at Penn State, got his accounting degree and went to work for some CPA firms in the Harrisburg area for a few years. He continued this in the winters after his family purchased Willow Mill Park in 1956.

It's said that Al knows where every nickel is that comes into and goes out of Funland, and his financial worksheets are a thing of beauty. He's never used a computer, having started doing the books long before the computer age and preferring to continue doing them the way he knows best. He is perhaps best known in the family for his comparisons, looking at things ranging from how individual rides and games do year after year to number of tickets sold, number of employees and much more. Computer or not, few people maintained books and financial records so thoroughly, especially back in the early days of Funland.

"A guy came into the office in 1972 flashing an IRS badge and said he was here for an audit," Al remembers. "So he came in, I set him up at a desk and brought him what he needed. When I brought him our books, he started to laugh. I said, 'I don't see what's funny?' He said, 'I came to Rehoboth several days ago and started at the north end of the boardwalk and have worked my way down, and you're the first one who has been able to give me any books.'"

In recent years, Al has turned over most of the financial work to Henschke and his daughter, Erin Darr, and Fiona Curry, who is married to Randy and Gwen Curry's son Ian. Though now doing everything on the computer, they continue to strive for the high standard Al set.

"I've never met anyone sharper from a financial perspective," Henschke said. "Over the years, I've saved a lot of the worksheets he's done. It's amazing how meticulous he is. One year I had payroll taxes; it was like three pages, and he scanned it and told me I was off by a couple of pennies. No adding machine, he just did it in his head. I said, 'You have to be kidding,' but he was right. Even today I do quarterly tax returns, but I take them all to him to check. And if I made a mistake, he always picks it up."

◆ ◆ ◆ ◆

The brothers live next door to each other in Hershey and see each other almost every day when both are in town. Their lives and their families have intertwined for so many years, and they are such family people that it seems rare to see them alone. Al is almost exactly 3½ years older than Don, and both brothers say they've had a good relationship through the years.

They grew up at a time shortly after the Great Depression and are loath to throw away anything that could possibly be used in place of purchasing something new.

"We used to have the old wooden boardwalk inside Funland," Don said. "When we took that out and started pouring the concrete, we always saved all the good boards and stacked them somewhere and reused them. We did not throw a lot away."

Their recycling tendencies did vary somewhat, though. When asked to confirm a story about whether he and his brother actually reused boardwalk nails after a storm, Don laughed and said, "He's the one who would straighten nails and reuse them. I never did that much."

The early years of Funland were a simpler time, in many ways. There were no job titles, no performance reviews and no rules for the family about the number of hours worked or doing more than one job. It was a matter of doing what needed to be done.

"One reason I think we didn't have more problems is because we each had an area we were responsible for, and we did that," Don said. "Al pitched in to help bring home a ride each winter, work on it, paint it, and he was right there helping with the rest of us. That spirit of teamwork has really helped over the years."

Incidentally, when I talked to Al in mid-January 2018, he mentioned that the next day he would be spending some time painting the Paratrooper, so this teamwork continues.

"He's been great to have around," Al says of his younger brother. "I have no mechanical skills, and he's excelled in that area, fixing the rides, which has been critical to our success. I think we've gotten closer since our wives have passed away. It's nice to have him right next door."

MY FUNLAND STORY: Roger Keyser (as told by his older brother, Wayne)

Our parents owned a summer house in Rehoboth, and we loved going to Funland and riding on the rides as kids. Roger was mildly retarded, what they would refer to as developmentally disabled today, and even as an adult he enjoyed spending time at Funland and getting to know the employees and the Fasnacht family that owns Funland.

Then one day, the Fasnachts offered Roger a job as a ticket shredder. He loved that job, and I'm very grateful to the Fasnachts for creating

Roger Keyser

a job for Roger to give him something meaningful to do. Roger loved wearing his Funland clothes and going to Nicola's for pizza with the staff on Sundays after work and being a part of the crew.

Funland was like a second home to Roger. It was everything to him because that job gave him both respect and a purpose. The Fasnachts and their employees treated Roger like any other person, and they looked out for him. You can't put a value on that.

Roger had quite a collection of Funland team photos from his years there. He wanted everyone to know he worked at Funland and was part of the Funland family. He so looked forward to the start of summer each year so he could return to Funland.

I will never forget that when Roger passed away in December 2011, several members of the Fasnacht family came to Roger's memorial service in Arlington, Virginia, just two days before Christmas. I was amazed, and it helped me better understand why Roger thought Funland was such a special place.

CHAPTER 4:

You're Not Working For Us, You're Working With Us

"People see the kids — our summer crew — running the rides and games, and they are key to our efforts to be good stewards, and good hosts, to our customers. The things we've done for our employees — housing them, feeding them, treating them to pizza and subs, playing sports with them and getting to know them — are all geared to making us feel like one big family."
— Al Fasnacht

Fasnacht family members and summer employees in 2008.

All families have to deal with issues from time to time. How people handle these situations is a good indication of what kind of people they really are. One of the first former Funland employees I interviewed for this book told me she stole money from Funland while working the games. I will call her "Sue," as she asked me not to use her real name. Stealing money is fairly easy to do at Funland if one is so inclined, as employees working the busy games are handling a lot of cash, and while you are supposed to put it in the change bag you wear around your waist — with all bills folded president-side out, with the $1 bills on the outside and the bigger bills inside – your pants pockets are very close and covered by the change bag, which aids in the deception.

Sue, who has battled drinking problems much of her life, said she thought for many years about coming clean to Al about her actions and apologizing. She worked up the nerve to tell him in the summer of 2017, as part of her recovery process. She went up to his office, which is on the second floor of Funland's main administration building, right behind the Kiddie Chair Swing and Jungle of Fun.

"I told him about stealing the money, and how sorry I was and that I was ready to start making payments for what I owed. My biggest fear was that he would be disappointed in me. I was crying my eyes out," Sue said. "He told me that people make mistakes and forgave me immediately without a question. I couldn't believe it. I stole from people I loved. He did not want any money. He just sat and talked to me and said the most important thing was that I stay sober. I was moved beyond anything. I left his office that day with a stronger bond with him than when I came in, which I didn't think was possible. He is an amazingly forgiving man."

Al said employees stealing money is a part of doing business, and that they have fired employees who were caught in the act. He recognized, though, that it wasn't easy for Sue to share her story.

"The fact that her conscience wanted her to try to make amends I thought took a great amount of courage," he said. "In visiting prison inmates – mostly lifers – as part of the prison ministry work I have done since the early 1980s, I know those people would all like a second chance. So it's just a matter of being able to forgive someone if they've done you wrong, because you've also done other people wrong. I don't hold grudges."

◆ ◆ ◆ ◆

Al always told new summer employees, "You're not working for us, you're working with us." He worked hard over the years – through actions and policies – to create a family-centric culture. Fasnacht family members wear the same uniform as the summer employees do, and Al expects the entire Fasnacht family to lead by example. This often took the form of a family member rushing in to handle an undesirable job, like taking out the trash, something many business owners would delegate to others.

"The biggest thing in being a leader is not asking your employees to do something you wouldn't do," Al said. "I've always made it a policy that if I hear of a throw-up, I jump in and clean it up. I guess it is called hands-on leadership. It's not that I like cleaning up a throw-up, but it sets a beautiful example.

"One particular story along these lines I will never forget: We had an employee named Teddy Mandes who was working the Tubs-O-Fun [which were metal tubs you sat in that had a wheel in the center. The wheel controlled how fast a tub would spin. The faster you turned the wheel, the quicker the tub would spin.] I was giving breaks, so I said, 'Teddy, it is your break time.' Just as I said that, someone leaned out over the ride and threw up all over my shoes. Teddy looked down, tried to keep from smiling and said, 'I will see you after my break, Al.'"

Cleaning up throw-up was the task employees dreaded more than any other. On some rides, especially those that spin or move quickly, this clean-up could entail covering quite a wide area. The first priority was to assist customers and help clean them up, followed by cleaning up the ride and ride area as thoroughly and quickly as possible. We typically put a cat litter-like substance on it, removed it with a dustpan and brush, used a towel to make sure the ride was clean, and then went back to running the ride. At night, some of the more common throw-up rides have two people assigned to them, so the person lower in seniority usually got this duty. As an aside, it always amazed me that people waiting to ride would see where this took place and would still rush to get into that car or seat before it was clean, as though nothing had happened. We had to tell people they could not ride in that car until it was clean.

"I remember one time while working one of the kiddie rides a child peed on the seat, and I asked Al, who just happened to be walking by, where I could get a bucket and a rag to clean it up," said Duane Kenney, a Funland employee the summers of 1992 and 1993. "He quickly came back with them, only to clean it up himself. I cleaned up my fair share of bodily fluids those two summers and never complained once, due to his example."

◆ ◆ ◆

I worked at Funland the summers of 1980 through 1985, and some of its unique, employee- and family-friendly policies demonstrated their belief in doing what they felt was the right thing, even if those actions negatively impacted the bottom line. Specifically:

- Employees lived rent-free in two dormitories when I worked there – one above the main

Life in the dorms above Funland included a hot dinner every day but Sunday.

park, where I stayed, and another above the Royal Treat, a breakfast and ice cream place at 4 Wilmington Avenue that opened in the summer of 1981.

- A dormitory "mother" cooked dinner for us six nights a week – all but Sunday – and did our laundry. The Fasnacht family provided milk, bread and peanut butter and jelly for sandwiches at other times of the day and night.

- On paydays, we received only a portion of our pay each week – $25 out of the $100 a week I earned in my first summer of 1980. The remainder was given to us in our end-of-summer check to ensure we would take home as much money as possible.

- An end-of-summer bonus based on our work performance and how much of the summer we worked also sent us home happy.

- Employees received free subs from Louie's on Rehoboth Avenue on Wednesday nights after work and free pizza and soda from Nicola's Pizza on First Street every Sunday night after work and our weekly employee meeting. Both were employee favorites, as I can clearly re-member how hungry I seemed to be every night after my shift ended.

- We enjoyed a weekly "anything goes" bumper car night, and members of the family often joined in and took much of the beating. Unlike while operating the ride during the day, when "one-way traffic" was the rule, no such rule applied to what was basically a free for all.

- The Fasnacht family organized employee-only tournaments on many of the games to determine bragging rights for the year. One former employee I talked to, Jimmy Lacey, who worked at Funland the summers of 2005 through 2011, had "Funland Skee-Ball Champion and Two-Time Funland Whac-a-Mole Champion" on the name badge he wore at Funland, and below his name on his email to me.

- Family members took us water skiing a couple of times a summer the years I was there. They also organized games of touch football and softball, Fasnacht family vs. employees, and the family was always out to win. In one softball game, a former employee was playing on the family team, and his pregnant wife was the center fielder. Al gave the summer crew a good-natured ribbing when it lost.

- The employees, all male, who lived in the dorms were split into two shifts, with one employee as shift supervisor, or King Shift (KS). On any given day one shift worked 1 to 5 pm, had 5 to 7 pm off for dinner, and then worked 7 pm until the park closed. The other shift did not start work that day until 5 pm – meaning employees got a beach day every other day – and worked from 5 pm to close. The shift starting at 5 pm would also sweep the park at night.

- Employees needed to be in the dorms by a certain time every night after work. The curfew was 2 am, or two hours after the last shift of employees got off for the night. The shift supervisor enforced the curfew. On some very busy nights, such as around the July 4 holiday or on non-rainy Saturday nights in August, curfew could be as late as 3 or 3:30 am. I served three years as KS, and staying up to check curfew every other night was not the most fun part of that role.

In getting to know other summer-only workers in Rehoboth, we learned our experience and the family atmosphere the Fasnacht family worked hard to create was the exception to the rule.

"Looking back, I don't know anywhere else where you got to live on the boardwalk, receive a hot meal each day, have a beach day every other day and still went home with money at the end of the summer," said Doug Reeder, who worked at Funland the summers of 1978 through 1982. "I had friends who had to work two or three jobs each summer just to live and work at the beach, and they went home with nothing but memories."

Employee tournaments are fun, competitive and a source of pride for the winner.

Living in the dorms – and knowing I didn't have to survive on my cooking and laundry skills – was very reassuring to my parents, and was also a preview of college life in some ways. There were as many as six bunks in a room, and the plywood walls served as more than barriers; they were a living Funland museum, loaded with names of former employees, artwork and sayings of years gone by. "Make love not war" is one I will always remember, etched during the Vietnam War years.

The dorm also had a TV in a large, open room with a laundry table, a long wooden table where we ate dinner, and the kitchen. This room also featured many large windows, which provided great views of the boardwalk, beach and Atlantic Ocean and was a regular hangout spot for us to check out the surf and to watch the world – and girls – go by. That togetherness built camaraderie and many lifelong friendships.

Those close quarters also led to pranks – usually called "pimpovers" – of all kinds, especially on first-year employees, known as "rookies," or "rooks," for short. Some of the more legendary pranks included getting unfilled jelly doughnuts from Garrison's Olde English Donut Shop on Rehoboth Avenue (no longer there), filling them with shaving cream and giving them to unsuspecting coworkers; flipping beds, which were really cots, with the occupant in them; hiding mattresses among the rides; putting peanut butter on someone's stomach, putting matches in the peanut butter, lighting them and putting a jar over the mix to form a tight seal; placing powders of all kinds of the back of fan blades, so that when the owner turned it on, he would get quite a dusting (since the dorms did not have air conditioning, most people had fans close to or suspended over the beds, making this prank very effective).

One of the most memorable pranks could aptly be described as horseplay. "In my first summer working at Funland, 1971, one of my coworkers took some modeling clay and used it to turn a horse on the Merry-Go-Round from a mare to a stallion," said Ron Murphy, who worked at Funland from 1971 through 1982. "This went unnoticed by staff for a couple of weeks."

When I moved into the dorm for the summer of 1980, there was no in-dorm shower. The one shower was outdoors, near the Funland office building and within 50 feet of a ride. So an employee would walk from the dorms down the steps next to the Merry-Go-Round and would have to go past all the kiddie rides. The tricky part, though, was walking back to the dorm after the shower, as some employees were looking to pull your towel off and embarrass you in front of whoever was in the park at the time. I learned the hard way to take clothes with me to change into for the return trip, and by my third summer there were showers in the dorms to prevent such mischief.

The biggest parental selling point about working at Funland – at least for my dad – was the guarantee of bringing home a sizable check. Employees received only a quarter of your weekly pay for living expenses. You could ask Al for more, but you'd better have a good reason. Otherwise, you were out of luck. Another life lesson learned. It's amazing how easy it was to live on $25 a week in spending money when everyone faced the same situation.

◆ ◆ ◆ ◆

Pizza night, held Sunday after work and an employee meeting, is a long-standing Funland tradition.

I was 16 my first summer working at Funland, and a big part of the experience for me was being on my own. Rehoboth Beach, like many summer resort communities, has long been a rite of passage for young seasonal employees away from mom and dad for the first time, which poses potential challenges for the employee, the employer and the city alike.

"We never worried about the kids that lived and worked at Funland, and that's a huge issue in Rehoboth," said Sam Cooper, Rehoboth Beach mayor from 1990 to 2017. "Kids get down here and, for many, it's the first time they've had the freedom of being out of the house and out from under mom and dad's control. And oftentimes not-so-good things happen, as they don't know their limits. I always felt those kids who worked for Funland had more supervision than a lot of other kids who worked in Rehoboth."

Rehoboth Beach's temporary summer workforce has taken on a much more international flavor in recent years as teens and twenty-somethings from Eastern European countries in particular have flocked to seaside towns as a way to experience the United States and work to pay their expenses. The temptations created by being so far from home and family, though, were very real no matter where you call home.

"We kept a close eye on how merchants treated their employees, particularly when they had young employees from overseas. Those kids tend to go wild when they get here," said John Hughes, Rehoboth Beach mayor from 1981 to 1987. "The vast majority of Funland's employees are only there in the summer, and they are at a volatile age where they could easily get into a world of trouble. The Fasnachts watch that stuff carefully, and I never had any hesitation to recommend a job at Funland to any young person because I knew it would be a formative period in their lives."

◆ ◆ ◆ ◆

With any group of mostly teenagers operating the rides and games all summer, there are bound to be some lapses in judgment that lead to experimentation and testing of the standard norms. This experimentation rarely escapes the Fasnachts' notice.

A guy I worked with for a number of years was notorious for pulling such stunts. One afternoon he was working Derby, the horse racing game on the boardwalk where you try to roll a red ball into holes with the numbers 1, 2 and 3. If the ball goes in a hole, your horse moves that many spaces. Derby has a specific soundtrack – the famous William Tell Overture – but that afternoon, he decided to play heavy metal music instead. That lasted for 15 to 20 minutes before a Fasnacht family member heard it and had him go back to playing the standard Derby musical accompaniment, composed by Rossini for the opera William Tell that premiered in Paris in 1829.

Another time that same summer, he was operating the Gravitron, a spaceship-looking ride that has padded panels along the perimeter, which are angled back, that riders lean back against. As the ride rotates, centrifugal force moves the panels up, lifting the riders off the floor in the process. The ride operator is seated in the ride's center, making sure everyone is safe and controlling the sound system. In this case, he turned the music up so loud it sounded like a rock concert, and the music could be heard throughout the park, probably for the first and only time. The concert lasted a couple of rides before he was told to cut it out.

It's no coincidence both of these incidents occurred in the afternoon, when, on sunny beach days, the park was at its slowest and boredom would sometimes creep in.

Torey Millman Hall, who worked at Funland the summers of 1995 and 1996, took it upon herself to drum up some business one night on the Sea Dragon, a ride shaped like a pirate ship that swings back and forth, the south side of which comes within a foot or two of hitting a house in which several Fasnacht families reside. The people at the far end of the pirate ship feel more effect from the angular momentum the ride generates, and there is often some yelling and screaming. Hall, though, wanted to amp that up a little.

"When everyone was seated on the ride and we were ready to go, I made an announcement for a game. When I point to your side, scream as loud as you can, and the side that screams the loudest wins," Hall remembers. "I then started the ride and pointed to the left side, and those riders screamed. I then pointed to the right side, and they screamed. Everyone was having a great time, and my line rapidly became full. This went on for about 20 minutes when I heard one voice over all the others. It was Al, and he was livid. He said, 'Stop making them scream. The neighbors are complaining.'

"I immediately stopped the game, and later, after the park closed, I apologized to Al. No longer mad, Al laughed about it and sent me on my way. So I took away three things from that situation, and from working for Al for two summers:

1. Al's love, sincerity and understanding of those who worked for him. He tolerated a lot from us kids.

2. Don't piss him off. Even without words, just one look with his steely blue eyes would reduce you to liquid.

3. Working with Al made it difficult to complain about our jobs. Here is this 70-year-old man [now 90 as of November 10, 2018] hustling along with us kids. If we sweat, he sweats, and he never asked you to do something he wouldn't do, or that we hadn't seen him do. He was no dictator boss; he was a participating boss. And that is a quality I've looked for in a boss in every job I've ever had. … Thank you for giving me the best summers of my life."

MY FUNLAND STORY:
Aaryn Zimmerman

In second grade, my best friend, Sadie, invited me to come with her and her family to Rehoboth Beach. I accepted the invitation and joined them for a week of fun. I fell in love with Funland the minute I saw it. The bright lights, smiling faces, games, rides and energy amazed me. The place felt like Heaven on earth! One invitation quickly turned into years of tradition.

Aaryn (right) with coworker Angelo Scanio.

One day during my last semester of high school, I came across an article in the Washington Post about working at Funland. The article said Funland was a place where memories were made, long-lasting friendships formed and life lessons learned. When my mom asked what I wanted to do the summer after high school, the answer was easy – work at Funland, which I did. That was the summer of 2013.

During my first semester of college, things took a turn for the worse. My health started rapidly declining, and doctors could not figure out what was wrong. I was exhausted after taking just a couple steps, I lost 50 pounds, my skin turned yellowish (anemia) and I had horrible night sweats. It got to the point where I had to use a wheelchair and change my sheets multiple times throughout the night because of the night sweats.

The following semester, doctors finally figured out I had stage-four cancer. This meant instead of returning to Funland in the summer like I had planned, I had to stay home and receive chemotherapy treatment. As you can imagine, I was heartbroken.

A couple months into treatment, I received the sweetest gift – a Funland family T-shirt and certificate, good for the following summer at Funland. The Funland family T-shirt is a prized possession, and not everyone has one. I was so grateful and thankful. I responded to treatment very well, which meant I could return to Funland the following summer.

My second summer at Funland [2015] was the best summer of my life. Less than a year earlier I thought my life was ending, and now I was given a second chance. I remember thinking to myself, this is how life should be.

Towards the end of the summer, friends and I threw a party. Alcohol was involved, and things got out of hand. No one got arrested or anything like that, but one girl showed up to work super hung over and sick the next day.

She actually puked at Funland, which made personnel manager Chris Darr very mad. All involved got in trouble with Chris.

I have never been so embarrassed in my life. Here was a family who had been so kind to me and had given me the chance to come back and work with the idea that I was a good worker and I blew it. It made me reflect on what kind of person I wanted to be. Did I want to be like the Funland family: Respectful, kind, caring, compassionate and loving? Or did I want to act like an idiot?

I am now studying medicine to become a pediatric oncologist. I use the lessons I learned while working at Funland to guide me. They have raised and loved me like I'm one of their own. They have been there for me through the hardest parts of my life and when I've made mistakes. They've taught me life lessons I will never forget. Funland raised me to be a good person, and for that, I am forever grateful.

CHAPTER 5:

Today's Fun at Yesterday's Prices

*"It costs the same amount of money to run a ride if there are
two people on it or 22 people on it, so why not keep the prices at a point
where more people can have enjoyment and give them the opportunity
to do more, and ride more rides, with their money?"*
— Al Fasnacht

Imagine owning a business, any business, and keeping your prices the same for 25 years. Now imagine if this is an amusement park, and the prices were the cost of ride tickets. Funland opened in 1962 selling ride tickets for 10 cents each or strips of 12 for $1. That pricing remained unchanged through the summer of 1986. According to the Bureau of Labor Statistics, 10 cents in 1962 had the buying power of 36 cents in 1986, and 83 cents in 2018, but that inflation was not reflected in the prices of the trademark green Funland ride tickets.

What did increase were the costs to keep the rides maintained and in good working order; the salaries for the employees who operated the rides; the cost of electricity to

*Funland has charged just one ticket for two rides —
the Boats and the Fire Engines — since opening in 1962.*

power the rides; the cost of liability insurance to protect the Fasnacht family in case of an accident; and many other expenses too numerous to mention.

Funland Ride Ticket Pricing History			
Years	Individual Ticket	Discounted Tickets	Discounted Cost Per Ticket
1962-1986	10 Cents Each	12 Tickets for $1	8.3 cents
1987-1995	20 Cents Each	12 Tickets for $2 35 Tickets for $5	16.7 cents 14.3 cents
1996-1998	25 Cents Each	18 Tickets for $4 54 Tickets for $10	22.2 cents 18.5 cents
1999-2005	25 Cents Each	24 Tickets for $5 54 Tickets for $10	20.8 cents 18.5 cents
2006-2012	30 Cents Each	48 Tickets for $12 90 Tickets for $20	25 cents 22.2 cents
2013-2014	35 Cents Each	48 Tickets for $14 100 Tickets for $25	29.2 cents 25 cents
2015-2017	35 Cents Each	50 Tickets for $15 100 Tickets for $25	30 cents 25 cents
2018-Present	40 Cents Each	50 Tickets for $18 100 Tickets for $30	36 cents 30 cents

Ticket prices in 1987 increased to 20 cents for individual tickets or a strip of 12 for $2. In 2018, individual Funland tickets cost 40 cents each, and you could buy 50 tickets for $18 (36 cents per ticket) or 100 tickets for $30 (30 cents per ticket). Compare that to some of Funland's closest seaside competition. At Trimpers in Ocean City, Maryland, individual tickets cost 60 cents in 2018, and you could buy 40 tickets for $20 (50 cents per ticket). Morey's Piers, which runs three amusement piers and two water parks with more than 100 rides on the boardwalk in Wildwood, New Jersey, sold individual ride tickets for $1.10 each and offered several discount ticket packages that could bring the cost as low as 70 cents each if you buy $180 worth of tickets all at once. In comparing the parks, it should be noted that Morey's and Trimpers are bigger and have more "thrill" rides for older kids and adults. By the same token, Funland charges fewer tickets per ride for similar rides than Morey's and Trimpers, and Funland has two rides – the Boats and the Fire Engines – that it charges only one ticket to ride. One-ticket rides at pay-as-you-go parks are about as rare as someone leaving the beach with no grains of sand.

"When you are at Funland you have the perspective of, 'I am not getting gouged.' I am the Midway Director at Circus Circus Hotel and Casino in Las Vegas, and we may be one of the biggest game operators in the country. And our prices have increased. Where can you ride a ride for 40 cents? You can't ride a mechanical horse outside of Walmart for that price," said Alan Kanter, who has worked in the amusement park industry for more than 35 years, including at Hersheypark. "Going to Funland is less expensive than going to the movies. And when you factor in the skill games as well, the prices they charge are likely the lowest and most cost-efficient in the country. I don't know anyone who charges as little as they do, and that is a reflection on Al. He wants people to come and have a good time."

❖ ❖ ❖ ❖

Almost all seaside parks – especially those on a boardwalk or pier – are not of the pay-one-admission-price variety that you tend to see at theme parks and most other amusement parks. That's because of the nature of the boardwalk, and the ebb and flow of people. Parks like Funland need to be able to bring people in without any kind of barrier. Some people actually walk through Funland on their way to or home from the beach, and I know from experience that even on perfect beach days, you would see kids, in particular, who were bored or didn't like the beach, talk their parents out of some money to spend on Funland games or rides. The fact that you could come as you are – sand, swimsuit and all – and hang out and pass some time doing something you've looked forward to since the previous summer for relatively little cash has a certain appeal to kids and parents alike.

Funland's pricing structure has always been set by Al, who said he learned the value of money from his German grandparents.

"I have always had a problem with situations that I look at as taking advantage of people," Al said. "I appreciate something that is reasonably priced and a good value, and we try to offer our customers the kind of experience, fun, entertainment and value that you'd like to have offered to you, with the same friendly relationship with the people who are serving you. We came up with the phrase, 'Today's fun at yesterday's prices' many years ago to describe Funland, and that is more important now than ever with the cost of a week at the beach higher than it has ever been. Families need to have places they can go as a group for affordable fun, and that is what we are all about."

Funland's famous green ride tickets have long been a great value.

While family members agree with providing affordable family fun, many feel ticket prices are too low and have told that to Al in family meetings and in other conversations. They argue that as employee salaries and the cost of new rides increase, so too should ticket prices.

"I've had many people ask me, 'How do you make money with that ticket price?'" said Randy Curry, who is part of the third generation. "We need to increase ticket prices a little bit over a period of time. Otherwise, we're going to get to a point where there is going to need to be a substantial increase."

Adds Al's oldest son, Craig: "There is an interesting tug-of-war going on within the family on our ticket prices. Dad wants to keep ticket prices as low as possible in order that we can still earn a comfortable living. And certainly none of us are starving; we are doing very well. But sometimes I think my father doesn't realize how much we spent on a new ride, game or other things, and we need to do something to raise revenue to cover that."

For perspective, Funland's newest ride, the SuperFlip 360, was purchased new in 2017 for about $500,000.

◆ ◆ ◆ ◆

Major decisions, like setting ticket prices, have long rested with Al. While he often seeks input from family members, he has the final word. "Our joke is that everyone's vote added up to one less than Al's," said Al's younger son, Neil. That is not the case so much anymore, but Al's influence is still very strong.

Craig said Al recently purchased another three years' worth of tickets, many of which come in packs of 50 and 100, based on current Funland ticket pricing. This basically ensures ticket prices won't increase until it is time to purchase more tickets. "He got us again," Craig said with a smile.

Al knows how much Funland customers appreciate the affordable ticket prices; he hears that from the parents of kids every night as he gives 15-minute breaks seven days a week for eight of the summer staff who are working the kiddie rides. More people than ever before recognize him as Funland's owner, due largely to a CBS Sunday Morning piece on Funland that aired in 2015. Many, though, have no idea of this friendly ride operator's role in the amusement park, which suits Al just fine.

"There's hardly a night that goes by that someone doesn't mention how much they appreciate our low prices," Al said. "They also tell me things like, 'We love Funland. Don't change a thing,' and 'We hope your family runs it forever.' It is a joy to hear things like that."

Karen Palmertree, for example, has been bringing her family to Rehoboth from Reading, Pennsylvania, for many summers and has seen three generations of her family – including her five grandchildren – experience the magic of Funland.

"It is amazing how low Funland's prices are, with prices everywhere else going up. There is not any place I can take my grandchildren that's more affordable," Palmertree said. "Funland brings smiles to my grandchildren's faces. My kids love taking their children to the place they loved as kids. We've made so many memories at Funland. I am smiling now, just thinking about our Happy Place."

◆ ◆ ◆

Many factors go into how much Funland charges for rides and games. As the owner of any viable business will tell you, the amount of money you bring in must exceed your expenses. The lower your overhead, the cheaper your prices can be to still make a profit. The Fasnacht family has made limiting expenses and costs a priority since its days running Willow Mill Park, and has continued that financial discipline at Funland.

The best example of this is the family's approach to perform virtually all the ride maintenance and upkeep, park repairs of any kind, and nearly all the jobs necessary for an amusement park to function, except for the employees it hires to work as ride and game operators. If something needs to be done, someone from the family is there to do it.

Funland spends no money on advertising and has a highly trained specialist in charge of trash detail and recycling – Al. He gathers all the trash and sorts the recycling the way Rehoboth collects it, seven days a week when Funland is open.

"When you have no skills, you do what's left," Al said with a smile when talking about his trash and recycling duties. "The reason I started doing the trash was because it was something I could do to carry my share of the load. So much of my life has been spent at Funland, and I'm very fortunate I'm still able to help. Let's face it, at my age, you're not supposed to lift 40 pounds of garbage. I want to be able to contribute and still be a part of something that means so much to me and my family."

◆ ◆ ◆

Funland's footprint is such that it really can't add a new ride or game without removing one. This means the stakes are higher at Funland to select a good ride that will increase the park's revenue as compared to parks with unlimited space. An added twist here is that the new ride or game is usually much more expensive than the one it is replacing. Such decisions are not hastily made and have often followed a similar path: Someone in the family, or a friend in the amusement park industry, sees a ride or game he or she thinks would be good for Funland. Oftentimes Al's initial reaction is one of caution, thinking, in part, that if this ride or game is such a winner, there is no rush to make a decision. Future reports will present a more accurate picture. The family then performs a cost-benefit analysis of sorts, projecting what the new item will bring in, how long it will take to pay it off and any other perceived benefits or drawbacks. At that point, a decision to buy may be seriously considered.

Take the case of the Derby, or horse racing game, which has occupied the northernmost spot on the boardwalk in front of Funland since 1982. Neil, who has been in charge of Funland's games since 1976, first looked into the game – made by Elton Amusements, Ltd., of Liverpool, England – several years earlier. He had received reports about its popularity from others in the industry. The price tag, though, was staggering – $65,000 – more than Neil paid for his house in Hershey. It would not be an easy sell.

"Paying that much for a game was unheard of for us," Neil said. "We kept hearing from others how popular it was, and we did a lot of investigating, and after a few years we made the decision to buy it. That was one of our best moves ever, as the game proved to be our most popular right away and has remained our top game every year since. Not only that, but adding Derby created a buzz among our customers, as it was something very different and had an appeal and charm that people could not get enough of."

Prior to the start of 2017, the Fasnacht family decided to replace the Super-Flip, arguably its most thrilling "thrill" ride, with a new and improved version, the SuperFlip 360. Unlike the original SuperFlip, which was a whirlwind of motion and featured three banks of rotating seats on an extending arm that, at its greatest length, spins high above the

The SuperFlip 360 is an investment in Funland's future.

park, the new and improved 360 version swings riders 360 degrees throughout the ride, hence the name. The SuperFlip 360 gives you an upside-down view of Funland from as high as 40 feet in the air.

One of Funland's ongoing challenges is having rides that interest older kids and adults. The park does not have the space for rides like roller coasters, so it tends to favor thrill rides that go up (in the air) instead of out, which require a bigger footprint. The Sea Dragon, a pirate ship that swings higher and higher, is another example. So while the SuperFlip 360's cost was a major consideration, other factors, such as Funland's viability in future years, played key roles in the decision to go with the new ride.

"When I look at the SuperFlip 360, I know it will take quite a few years for us to get our money out of that," Al said. "That's the chance you have to take and the thing you have to do – keep upgrading and give customers a new experience. One of the appealing features of that ride is it entertains those people who are standing there watching it. People really seem to like it, and we've had nights where the line was so long I thought we'd be running that ride until 1 or 2 am."

◆ ◆ ◆ ◆

Funland has been known to stay open that late occasionally – it has no official closing time – more to please customers than to make money – as there are usually only a few people on the last few rides of the night. Al is all about the customer experience, and as that relates to ticket prices, he feels lower prices mean more people have more fun, and what's so bad about that?

"I think providing the service we do lends itself to a great way to work," Al said. "The enjoyment you get from other people enjoying what you're providing is a great feeling. I don't want us to have a selfish attitude when it comes to ticket prices. Keeping our prices affordable is a way for us to give back for all that we have been given. We have been incredibly fortunate."

MY FUNLAND STORY: Mercedes Legget

We are recent transplants to the area – we moved to Milton, Delaware, in the summer of 2016 to open a restaurant called Cantina Ultima – and we kind of stumbled upon Funland that summer. We hadn't walked the whole boardwalk yet, and so we made a right at Rehoboth Avenue and were wandering down, and we noticed Funland. We kind of peeked around, and they have so much tucked into this small space. They utilize the space so creatively, and you go past the kiddie rides, and there are rides for older kids and grownups and arcade games.

I told the kids I would buy tickets and that they could ride two rides, because I thought it was going to be like the boardwalk in New Jersey where it costs an arm and a leg. I came back from the ticket booth and told the kids they could ride as many rides as they want. My husband said, "What do you mean?" and I said, "The tickets are like 30 cents." That's just insane.

I think it is a gem in a resort area that is really for all ages. It's a piece of Americana history that is still alive and running today.

It was not something I would have expected, to find someplace that has as much going on as they do with the great choice of rides and for it to be so inexpensive. As the parent of two kids, I especially love that. We spent eight hours riding rides and grabbing slices of pizza nearby and then going back to riding rides and playing games. At that point I had kids who were 10 and 11, and it was an amazing summer experience that all of us will always remember.

CHAPTER 6:

Five Rides Older Than Funland

*"The amusement park business is about making memories. Nostalgia is a
big part of that. By having five rides still operating since Funland opened
in 1962, you get the sense nothing has changed, and that it's timeless.
It's also generational. You went on those rides, you put your kids on those
rides and they put their kids on those rides. There's a lot to be said for that."*
– Alan Kanter, Midway Director at Circus Circus Hotel and Casino in Las Vegas

One of Funland's five oldest rides, the Boats have been producing smiles since long before 1962.

The Fasnacht family's purchase of Sport Center from the Dentino family
in the spring of 1962 included 12 rides, five of which – the Merry-Go-
Round, the Boats, Fire Engines, Sky Fighters and Helicopters – are still in
operation today. These five rides – all which debuted at Sport Center, with
at least one dating back to the mid-1940s – are mentioned time and again
by Funland customers as the ones three and four generations of their families
have enjoyed, contributing greatly to the park's timeless feel and the memories such shared experiences create.

"A lot of people comment on the fact that so much changes in life, and
that it is good to see something, like Funland, that basically stays the same,"

Al said. "And those five rides we've had since the beginning play a big role in that. I had a gentleman in the summer of 2017 tell me that he remembers riding on our Fire Engines 70 years ago, as he was putting a grandchild on the same ride. Helping families create those kind of memories is a good feeling and is at the core of what we've been trying to provide our customers since the beginning."

The section of Funland where four of these five rides reside – all but the Helicopters – has changed little since the late 1940s. The Merry-Go-Round, Boats, Fire Engines and Sky Fighters are all right next to each other, and many kids go from one to another, with their loved ones trying to keep up every night of their vacation. This is known as the "Row," a collection of smiles, noises, crowds, laughter, photos and memories that is perhaps unequaled anywhere in Rehoboth Beach. The story of these rides is an interesting one that few, if any, of the hundreds of thousands of people who visit the park each summer have known much about. Until now.

◆ ◆ ◆ ◆

There is little doubt the Fire Engines are the oldest, and longest-running, of Funland's rides. Al said the Dentino family started putting in kiddie rides sometime shortly after World War II, around 1946. That timing aligns with the man he spoke to in 2017 who said he remembers riding the Fire Engines in 1947.

What is known about the Fire Engines is they were built by the Pinto Brothers, who, according to the Coney Island History Project, operated an amusement park factory on West 8th Street in Coney Island, New York, that focused on rides for kids. Silvio and Albert were the actual Pinto brothers, and their father, Silvio Sr., and cousin, Henry, were also a part of the business. The Fire Engines were just one of the rides made by the Pinto Brothers, as their ad in The Billboard magazine on November 24, 1951 indicates:

PINTO BROTHERS
For the finest in kiddie rides
KIDDIE FIRE ENGINE RIDE
KIDDIE PONY CART RIDE
2940 WEST 8th ST., CONEY ISLAND 24 N.Y.

The Pinto Brothers are best known for owning the famous Cyclone roller coaster in Coney Island for a number of years. Coney Island was once home to several large seaside amusement parks, including Dreamland, Luna Park and Steeplechase Park, earning it the nickname "The Nation's Playground." The Cyclone, along with the Parachute Jump and Wonder Wheel, perhaps best symbolized that booming amusement-park era in this section of Brooklyn from the late 19th century to the early 20th century, prior to World War II.

Built in 1927, the Cyclone was a precursor to the thrill or action rides seen today. A wooden roller coaster, the Cyclone reaches speeds of 60 miles per hour and, according to the New York City Department of Parks and Recreation, is the second-steepest wooden coaster in the world with a drop of 85 feet at an angle of 58.1 degrees. The Cyclone's ties to roller coaster history go deeper still, as it is on the same site where the first coaster designed as an amusement park ride in the United States, the Switchback Railway, was built in 1884.

According to The New York Times, Silvio Pinto and his family owned and operated the Cyclone for a number of years before selling it to New York City for $1 million in 1971.

Al is unsure how old some of the rides they acquired from the Dentino family were when his family purchased Sport Center. When it applied for an amusement license, the Fasnacht family had to list the year each ride was built, which Al said resulted in an educated guessing game. He is more confident, though, about how the Fire Engines ended up in Rehoboth.

"The Pinto Brothers both built and operated rides," Al said. "In the off-season they would build a kiddie ride, and then they would encourage amusement park people to visit in the summer to see it. If they liked what they saw, they would place an order to have it built during the next winter. I know that's how we got the Fire Engines."

Regardless of how this ride came to be, customers are glad this oldest of Funland rides is still going strong.

"Funland is near and dear to my family," says Mary Slogosky, of Philipsburg, Pennsylvania, who has vacationed in Rehoboth for more than 30 years. "It is a big deal when a child in the family rides the Fire Engines for the first time. Our oldest is now 10, and when we stopped going to the kiddie-ride side of the park, it actually brought tears to my eyes. I can't wait to get back on that side of the park with my grandchildren."

◆ ◆ ◆ ◆

Three of Funland's five oldest rides were built by the Allan Herschell Company, which opened an amusement park ride factory in North Tonawanda, New York, midway between Buffalo and Niagara Falls, in 1915. Best known for making hand-carved carousels, or merry go rounds, the Herschell Company made more than 3,000 of them, more than anyone else in the industry, and of which more than 100 are still in operation today, according to the Herschell Carrousel Factory Museum (HCFM), which uses the French spelling of carousel. More facts from the HCFM: Around 1928, production of Herschell's carousel horses went from all wood to having horses with aluminum legs. The move away from wood and to aluminum continued with heads, and then tails. These horses, with wood bodies and aluminum heads, tails and legs, were referred to as half-and-halfs.

Starting in 1950, Herschell's carousel horses were made entirely out of aluminum. Al said Funland's Merry-Go-Round was purchased by the Dentino family in 1960, so its horses are made of aluminum. The Billboard magazine, in its "RIDES – What's on the Market" list that appeared on April 11, 1960, listed the purchase price for the type of merry-go-round Funland has at between $31,750 and $34,750, which would be about $275,000 in 2018 dollars.

The damage from the Great Atlantic Storm of 1962 ended right at the edge of where the Merry-Go-Round was, a fortunate break as that meant the ride still had a roof. What it didn't have during Funland's first summer was any protection from the sea air blowing in off the Atlantic Ocean. To make matters worse, that winter another powerful Nor'easter carried the roof covering the Merry-Go-Round from its supporting walls about 100 feet, over the roofs protecting the other kiddie rides, and slammed it against and into the house at the back end of Funland that also served as the office. All this damage was repaired in time for the next summer.

The Merry-Go-Round has occupied virtually the same space in the center of Funland since at least 1962.

The Merry-Go-Round is one of the only rides that young kids, parents, grandparents and people of any age can ride together – or by themselves, for that matter.

"My daughter, Willow, has this one horse that she has to get on every time we go. That horse has a star on the back of its hip that says, 'Rehoboth Beach Patrol,'" says Shelly McHenry-Farmery, who has been coming to Funland for 42 years. "I rode on this same ride when I was a kid, and now to ride on it with my daughter and share those memories with her is just so cool. That's one of the reasons Funland is the ultimate family tradition."

◆ ◆ ◆ ◆

The Merry-Go-Round wins the award for the toughest kiddie ride to operate, or at least it did back in the 1980s when I worked at Funland. At that time, there were no gates around the ride; people could hop on at any time, and usually did. You had to constantly take a 360-degree look to make sure you weren't going to start the ride as someone was trying to get on, often with a little child. That person getting on would signal to others that they could, too, so sometimes it could take several minutes before I felt comfortable starting the ride safely. The ride operator would press a bell to indicate to everyone the ride was about to start, but oftentimes customers interpreted that as a last call to board.

Once the ride started, the real fun began. That's when you would leave the center of the ride where the controls were, which was not moving, and get onto the ride to collect tickets. You would walk in the opposite direction the ride was moving so you could approach riders the way they were facing to ask for their tickets. This took some getting used to and led many of us to grab onto a pole or horse to maintain our balance from time to time.

New riders usually had no idea tickets were collected during the ride – kids would often walk into the center area where I was standing before the ride started to hand me their tickets – and it sometimes created interesting balancing acts for parents, who were trying to hold on to their young children and the horse while reaching in their pockets for tickets. When you had a full ride, it could be a challenge to collect all ride tickets before it ended. On those occasions, the kids would search me out after the ride to make sure I received their tickets.

When I operated the Merry-Go-Round on sunny beach days, I was also responsible for running the Boats at the same time. This has not been the practice for many years, and is hard for most people to believe when talking about the old days at Funland. The way this worked was I would start the Merry-Go-Round, collect all the tickets and jump off while it was running to start the Boats. Jumping off the Merry-Go-Round took some practice, as it does anytime you move from something in motion to something that isn't. I can remember falling a couple of times, not exactly the look you wanted to instill confidence in the parents of kids nearby who were waiting to ride.

Watching two rides at once wasn't easy, and since the Boats usually had very little kids, you always stayed seated at that ride as it posed the greater danger. What that means is there was no realistic way to stop the Merry-Go-Round quickly in case of an emergency. I didn't think anything was unusual about this double ride duty during my six summers working in the park. Looking back, though, it seems like a minor miracle that no one was hurt or that I never received one question or comment about this practice.

◆ ◆ ◆ ◆

Carousels, though, were just one of many rides made by Herschell, which in industry ads in the 1940s and 1950s described itself as the "World's Largest Manufacturer of Amusement Rides." The list of rides Herschell manufactured include the Sky Fighters and Helicopters, both still going strong at Funland, and many other rides for kids such as miniature trains, roller coasters for kids and kiddie car, tank and boat rides, to name just a few. Herschell also made thrill rides for adults, such as the Sky Wheel, a double Ferris wheel almost 100 feet tall, and the Twister.

Herschell is also known for coming up with the concept of a "Kiddieland," the idea of grouping a bunch of rides together for small children. Funland's Kiddie Row is a good example.

The Sky Fighters were built in 1956.

The Sky Fighters are the oldest of the three rides. According to the serial number on the ride, it was manufactured in 1956. The price for a new Sky Fighters in 1960, according to The Billboard magazine, was between $5,900 and $6,500, so it likely would have been somewhat cheaper depending on the year it was purchased.

This ride features eight metal fighters, with seats facing forwards and backwards, for a seating capacity of 16. Riders reach a "cruising altitude" of 6½ feet during the ride, and they can "shoot" realistic machine guns that make noise and can be pointed in different directions. For bigger riders, there is not a lot of clearance between the top of their heads and the big green doors above the ride when those garage-style doors are open.

◆ ◆ ◆ ◆

The Helicopters are the reason several members of the Fasnacht family visited Sport Center, a visit that led to the creation of Funland. What made the Helicopters unique at the time was it was one of the first rides in which the riders, and not the ride operator, controlled the ride's movement. The Helicopters have a bar you hold on to. When you pull the bar in towards you, the helicopter goes up; when you push the bar away from you, the helicopter goes down. Based on my recent visits to Funland, young kids today enjoy being the pilot as much now as they did back in the 1980s.

Al believes the Dentinos purchased the Helicopters in 1961 – the sales price of a new Herschell Helicopters ride in April 1960 was between $10,750 and $11,500, according to The Billboard magazine, which would be about $90,000 in 2018 dollars – so it was a virtually new ride when Funland opened in 1962.

This was one of my favorite rides as a kid. Having control was key, and I remember feeling like I was so high off the ground and able to see so much of the park. I also remember moving the bar very quickly in and out, causing the helicopter to jerk up and down. This, I would quickly learn, was a no-no (it is hard on the ride's hydraulic system). I dealt with many kids like me years later as a ride operator, trying to cajole them – and often their parents stationed around the ride – to move the bar more slowly. I also enjoyed taking both my kids on the Helicopters and sharing this experience with them.

The Helicopters could also get very hot on a warm sunny day, especially the metal seats, and unsuspecting riders could be in for a surprise as they ran to select their helicopter and climbed aboard. All in all, though, this was a good ride to operate from an employee's perspective: you were in the sun, there were few issues, people did not get sick on the ride, and you were in the center of the park, which provided a good view of everything happening around you. When the weather was bad, the ride would often close, and you would be assigned to another ride to help someone else, which wasn't too common during the day and was a nice change of pace.

◆ ◆ ◆ ◆

That brings us to the Boats. This ride was made by Smith & Smith, Inc., of Springville, New York, and may well have been one of Sport Center's first rides. The Boats are often the first ride very young kids experience, as they can ride with an older sibling or friend and be perfectly safe. The Boats are still the originals, although the boat pond has been rebuilt once. They are painted every few years and touched up as needed, but look no worse for wear.

Another unique feature is the cost to ride. The Boats, along with the Fire Engines, have required only one ticket to ride since Funland opened in 1962.

◆ ◆ ◆ ◆

That these five rides have withstood the test of time so well is no surprise. Their simplicity is a big factor, as is the fact the family members who maintain the rides know virtually everything about them. Keeping them running, though, is just the start; it's also about making them as special as possible for all the families who have yet to experience them, as well as for those coming

Keeping Funland's older rides looking good requires work, such as giving them a paint job every now and then.

back for more.

"There is something about the way they maintain those kiddie rides and make them gleam," Kanter, the midway director at Circus Circus in Las Vegas, said. "They always have their rides gleaming, and they take so much pride in making sure everything is perfect. It's not like they think, 'We're getting ready to close so let's not worry about it.' They don't have that mentality; their mentality is that they should be perfect every day."

These rides form the heart and soul of Funland. They are where memories start being created for many families, and are rekindled and added to with each new generation.

"One of the powerful things about amusement parks are the emotions they convey," said Jim Futrell, historian for the National Amusement Park Historical Association, who has written multiple books on amusement parks. "At one end of the spectrum is the magic of Disney, and at the other end are parks like Funland that have been around for generations where parents can take their kids on the same rides they rode on when they were kids. Those shared, cross-generational experiences are one of the things that makes Funland so special."

Could these rides still be producing smiles and making memories if and when Funland turns 100 in 2061? Don't bet against it. "It's great to have the ability to tear these rides apart and to mechanically see how things are working and going," Randy Curry said. "To know that the rides have now lasted almost 60 years, with a little tender loving care, I could see them lasting another 60."

MY FUNLAND STORY:
Shelly McHenry-Farmery

I am 42 and have never missed a season at Funland. My daughter, Willow, is getting to live a part of what my childhood was. We rode on the same rides. Whatever ride she is on, say the Motorcycles, I remember that I had to be on the green metallic motorcycle, and my sister had to be on the purple one. Those were our colors.

I know what Funland smells like. It just says summer to me. It is a mix between the salt air and the rides at Funland that just say, "Hey, I am home for the summer." I could pinpoint that smell anywhere. It is the best smell ever. I love it. I could

Willow has spent part of every summer at Funland.

be a block away, and I can smell it. I can hear the screams in the air, and I know exactly where I am.

We live in Frenchville, Pennsylvania, which is just north of State College, and we get to Rehoboth one week a month between May and September. We come to Funland every night we're here, and it never gets old. We talk about Funland all the time. I have tickets all throughout my car, and I am working on a picture frame where I am outlining the background mat in Funland tickets and will include photos of Willow on the rides.

My mom lives in Dewey Beach, and Willow calls her every week. Every time she calls her, she will tell her how she did in school, like, "I got a 100 percent on my spelling test." And so my mom puts money into a jar for her to buy Funland tickets. We go down to see my mom, and she says, "Hey, here is your present." And it is Funland tickets. It is something you know we are going to use. They will never go to waste. The green Funland ticket, I have that on my key chain right now. Funland is just so much fun!

CHAPTER 7:

The RoyAl Treat

"The arrangement has never been in writing.
There's no lease. It is a handshake deal."
– Al Fasnacht

Ed Fornwalt and Al outside the Royal Treat.

Handshake deals are the stuff of legends, details added to stories to emphasize how one's word is their bond. The fact remains that due largely to common sense, such tales are the wishful transactions of fiction. In the case of the Royal Treat, the breakfast and ice cream parlor at 4 Wilmington Avenue that has become a Rehoboth Beach institution, though, a handshake in 1981 is the closest thing to a contract you will find.

Let me digress. In 1976, the Fasnacht family purchased what was the Royalton Hotel at 4 Wilmington Avenue, primarily to prevent any expansion of the commercial businesses on the boardwalk between Wilmington and Delaware Avenues. The 3½-story property had great bones but was no gem; it had been condemned by the town fire marshal because it did not come up to code. Meanwhile, senior citizens in Rehoboth were looking for a temporary home, as they were building a new facility a few blocks away. Al talked with the town about allowing the seniors to use this property after his family made some repairs, and the town agreed, with a few stipulations: they could use just the first floor and be there only during daylight hours.

Once the seniors moved to their new digs, the question of what to do with this well-situated property less than 100 yards from the beach was back. It was a longtime friend of Al's, Roy Edward Fornwalt, who goes by Ed, who made the best offer.

"Ed asked me, 'What would you think about the Fornwalt family operating a breakfast and ice cream parlor there?'" Al said. "Knowing Ed's background, initially a teacher and football coach and then as an estimator for a plumbing contractor, I figured he was well-qualified to run a restaurant. So I said, 'Sure, go ahead.'"

◆ ◆ ◆ ◆

Fornwalt had spent the previous 30 years in the mechanical engineering business and was ready for a change. He used to visit several New Jersey beaches, and after a tour of Rehoboth, he felt a breakfast and ice cream place could do well.

"I knew Al had to do something with the building, so I said, 'Let's work together on the thing. I'll make a business out of it, and you can house some of your workers in the rooms upstairs,'" Fornwalt said. "All of this was done by handshake, and we've been there now 37 years. Our relationship was and is very good, and we had no questions or problems whatsoever with a hand-shake deal. Those days are gone forever, that's for sure."

Adds Al: "The modern thought on a handshake deal is that it is crazy. Ed has a neighbor, a longtime resident of Hershey who is also a lawyer, and we all know each other. He went to talk to her about something years ago, and they got to talking about Ed's arrangement. When he told her it was a handshake deal, she shook her head and said, 'Who owns the building?' And Ed said, 'Al Fasnacht.' She said, 'Well, that explains it.' I took that to mean she had high regard for both of us."

◆ ◆ ◆ ◆

Their agreement has an interesting side clause: Al would do the Royal Treat's books, while Ed would be the Fasnachts' plumber. They helped each other in many ways. For several years when the Royal Treat first opened, Neil Fasnacht offered Funland employees incentives to make as much money as possible while working a shift at a game. If you met certain goals, you received coupons redeemable at the Royal Treat. This was not a motivation for every-one, but it certainly was for me. I love both breakfast and ice cream, and I had a lot of chances to work the games, especially at night. My favorite was Derby, the horse racing game, where on a busy Saturday night, you would regularly have 12 players from 7 to 11 pm, and often later. So if you could shave even 10 seconds off the time between games, over five hours you would collect a lot more money at 50 cents a player. I remember eating many free meals at the new establishment – my favorite breakfast is French toast with sausage and go-to dessert is the dusty road sundae – but I didn't realize at the time the Fasnachts were doing this to generate business for their friends during those crucial first few years of a restaurant. They needn't have worried.

"When we first started, I said we needed to give ourselves five years," Fornwalt said. "In those days, a business like ours in Rehoboth was only open about 120 days, and it sometimes took people a few summers to find you. But, before the end of our third year, we knew it was going to work, and the rest is history."

The two businesses, run by former football teammates at Hershey High School who were inducted into the school's athletic Hall of Fame in successive years, have a lot in common. Both are throwbacks to an earlier time – owners of a small family amusement park and an ice cream parlor that serves most of its concoctions in glassware – with a desire to provide affordable family fun. Think that's not possible for a breakfast and ice cream place? Try sitting on one of the Royal Treat's two screened porches and enjoying pancakes, or a sundae, with family or friends.

Speaking of tall tales, there's one surrounding how the Royal Treat got its name. It's been reported that Royal is an amalgam of Fornwalt's given first name, Roy, with Fasnacht's first name, Al. Makes for a great story: two friends for more than 70 years with both of their given names on the marquee. Alas, the real story is not as interesting. "I came up with the name Royal Treat," Al said. "My thinking was to name it after the Royalton Hotel, which stood on this property for many years. I had never heard the story about our names. I wish that were true." What is true is that the Royal Treat serves – you guessed it – Hershey's ice cream.

MY FUNLAND STORY:
Jan Patterson

I'm 44 years old, and my memories of Rehoboth Beach, the boardwalk and Funland extend back to my childhood years. My family and I visited Rehoboth from our home in southeastern Pennsylvania every summer. Funland was the "center of the universe" for me as a kid and teen vacationing at Rehoboth Beach.

Jan Patterson (sunglasses) and his family outside of Funland.

Thirty-plus years later, as a husband and father of two children living in Clarksburg, Maryland, Funland is still the "center of the universe" for me at Rehoboth, albeit for different reasons: low ticket prices, the rides and games, and the ultra-clean, and family-friendly, atmosphere.

That said, I still feel a bit nostalgic whenever I walk into Funland with my wife and children, or sit at the Derby for a few games and inhale the aromas and listen to the sounds of the rides, games and laughter. Most nostalgic for me, though, is watching my children have the same experiences and enjoyment at Funland, often with wide-eyed wonderment, that I did. I've carried my absolutely exhausted, sometimes crying son and daughter out of there on more than one occasion, a clear indication they had a great time and didn't want to leave, which is the same way I felt all those years ago.

As an aside, two summers ago an older man called out to me from the rocket ship ride because I was wearing a Penn State T-shirt (I'm a Penn State graduate, class of 1996). Turns out that was Al Fasnacht, patriarch of the Funland family and also a Penn State graduate. We talked about Penn State for a bit before the conversation drifted to Funland. I asked him why, at his age and stage of life, he was still working the rides and taking out the trash (yes, I saw him taking out the trash). He simply told me he does it because he loves doing it. He also described, with a twinkle in his eye, putting generations of family members on the same rides over the decades. My kids and I certainly fall into that group.

CHAPTER 8:
The Flying Cages

"The Flying Cages was THE ride all us guys wanted to work on. Could it have been because this is where the girls hung out? Or did they hang out at the Cages because of us? I choose to remember it being the latter."
– Jim Vienneau, Funland employee the summers of 1974 and 1975

The Flying Cages served as the backdrop for the 1972 Funland employee team photo.

One of the biggest draws to working at Funland for me and many others was spending the summer at the beach and meeting girls. Rehoboth has long been known as a resort frequented by many teenagers, who were the same age as the summer Funland employees. That dynamic played out every day at the park, especially on the thrill rides geared to older kids. And perhaps no ride in Funland history has generated more thrills than the Flying Cages.

The Cages were unique in that the rider(s) and ride operator generated all the power. The rider(s) would get in the big metal, rectangular cage, which had a bar on the inside on both the front and back sides for riders to hold on to, and a Funland employee would give the Cage a big push. At that point it was up to the rider(s) to shift their weight back and forth in an attempt to get the Cage to go "Over the Top." Once someone mastered the weight shift necessary to make this happen, the Cage would go around faster and faster, to the point where it appeared to be flying.

Getting the Cages flying was sort of an unofficial skill required of all Funland employees. We could ride any ride for free on our nights off, but the

61

Cages was by far the most popular, and a great way to demonstrate our talent for all onlookers. I remember one employee riding the Cages nonstop during our dinner break from 5 to 7 pm, and frequent contests among employees to see who could get their cage going the fastest.

"Riding the Cages on a night off was a must," remembers Ron Murphy, who worked at Funland for 11 summers in the 1970s and 1980s. "It gave us a chance to show off because most of the workers there could get the Cages going pretty fast. Another thing some of us did when starting off and getting to the top at a slow speed was reaching out and grabbing the support beam holding us in place at the top. This, of course, was a very big no no because if you didn't know what you were doing you could get seriously injured, and we didn't want customers trying to copy us."

Adds Jim Vienneau, "The Cages made us teenagers feel like we had man strength. The Funland guys would challenge all comers (park visitors) to races on our nights off. I never saw a Funland guy come close to being beat. It was not uncommon for us to do 50 or more revolutions before others could make it around once. We could turn those things into gravity torture devices like they used to punish astronauts in training."

The ride made its Funland debut in the summer of 1965 – the Fasnacht family purchased three Cages that year, and added three more in 1968, and was very popular right from the start with workers and customers alike. The Cages, though, had one big drawback – injuries, to both riders and the Funland employees doing the pushing. Riders who did not know how to make the Cage go over who rode with those that did were at most risk. They would not know how to shift their weight properly, and as the Cage got going faster and faster, they would find it very difficult to hold on. If they let go, they would bang around in the Cage until the ride operator could stop it, which we did with a big brake. Another problem was for riders who knew what they were doing but got tired, and would lose their grip. The result would often be cuts and scrapes, and sometimes broken bones. For ride operators, the temptation to give as big a push as possible could lead to problems.

"We had a constant battle with the kids trying to push it – we wanted them to just get the Cage going, and they wanted to give a huge push," Al said. "The problem was, the kids would get in under the Cage when giving a big push, and we had a kid who could not get out of the way and he broke his pelvis. The number of accidents we had on that ride were primarily due to people getting tired due to the exertion, and they would let go of the bar and would collapse and turn or break an ankle, twist a knee, that kind of stuff. And finally the insurance company said, 'we can't carry coverage on that ride any longer,' so that led to our getting rid of them [after the summer of 1983]."

The Flying Cages stories, though, will live on forever.

"My best memory was when a young lady was in the Cage in the mid-1970s, when tube tops were popular with girls," said Alan Houde, who worked at Funland in 1974 and 1975. "As she was going around the tube top began to slip down. We yelled at her not to let go of the bar. Eventually the top completed its journey downward and exposed its attributes. It was also the longest period of time on record for the pusher to be able to apply the brake and bring the cage to a stop. Good times at Funland."

MY FUNLAND STORY: Sam Blitz

Below is a letter Sam Blitz wrote to Funland at the age of 6 in 2018. Sam lives in New York City, but his grandmother, Judy, has a house in Rehoboth, and Sam has visited Rehoboth, and Funland, every summer of his life.

Did you ever go on a ride that lights up? Did you ever go on a gravatron? I think Funland is a super fun amusement park!

One reason is there are really colerful rides. Did you know there is also cool rides? It is so fun! Do you want to go?

Another reason is there is spektakeler games. As a matter of fackt, It is soooooooooo exciting! There is a game called the super drop. On the super drop you throw a ball in a hole with a number. The number you get is the amount of tickits you get. You should try to get the JACKPOT! In the Jackpot, it is possible to get 1,000 tickits!

Sam Blitz with Al, summer of 2018.

P.S. you should go. In addition there are even bumper cars!!!!!!

Did you know there is a hanted house? You should defenetley go. I think Funland is a super fun amusement park. It has really fun rides, there are spektacleler games, and there are even bumper cars. If you want to have a good time, go to Funland!

CHAPTER 9:
Joining the Family Business

"Al made it known right away that you had to do your share of the work, and you had to take on the bad jobs as quickly as the good jobs. There were not going to be any free rides."
– Bill Henschke, a third-generation family member

Bill Henschke has been working on Funland's Bumper Cars since 1977.

When Bill Henschke officially joined the family business in April 1977, he said he did not know what he was getting into. That feeling would not last long.

"The first job Al gave me was digging a trench under where the bumper car floor is now," remembers Bill, who is married to Al's daughter, Gail. "We were building a building on Brooklyn Avenue at the time. And he gave me a grain shovel, which is considerably wider than a normal shovel. I had to dig this trench about 3 feet deep and 3- to 4-feet wide, and it was not easy going through the sand with this shovel. I can remember thinking that he was giving me a heads-up here that you've got to work if you're going to join the Funland family, because I could have used a regular shovel and it would have been a lot easier, but he gave me the hardest one to make me work. He instilled a work ethic in me and other family members that has been a big part of our success."

Al has long said any family member is welcome to join the business as long as that person wants to work. There are no tests, trial periods or screenings of any kind; you just need to carry your share of the load. Amazingly, given the number of family members who have worked at Funland over the years, that has pretty much always been the case. Those in the family business are also expected to set an example for the summer crew.

"When the kids see how hard our family works, the ones that want to make an effort to work the way we want them to will follow suit," Al said. "Several years ago, I asked a member of our summer staff, who was from Eastern Europe, what he found different in America. One of the things he said was, 'In my country, the boss does absolutely no work, none. Here, your family works just like everyone else.' It impressed him."

◆ ◆ ◆ ◆

The decision of Al and Don's kids, the third generation who are now in their 50s and 60s, to join the family business was not assumed or required. While Al's and Jean's kids, Gail, Craig and Neil, all signed on soon after college and have stayed ever since, Don's and Dee's kids – Gwen, Lee Ann, Lisa and Amy – have done things differently. Gwen and her husband, Randy Curry, joined the family business early on. Lee Ann, after graduating from Susquehanna University in Selinsgrove, Pennsylvania, soon found a job with the federal government as a computer programmer at the Army Depot in Mechanicsburg, Pennsylvania, where she worked for 31 years before retiring in 2012. Lisa became a registered dietitian soon after graduating from Hood College in Frederick, Maryland, and worked at a hospital near Hershey for several years. When her husband, Brad, got out of the Coast Guard, where he received training in electronics, they decided to join the family business in 1986. Amy, who also graduated from Hood, went to work as the activities director on a skilled nursing unit after college. Several years after she married Steve Hendricks, who worked at Funland the summers of 1976 and 1977, they joined the family business in 1990. Amy and Steve left after 17 years, in 2007, in part so Amy could pursue a career as a marriage and family therapist.

Craig was drawn to electronics and was an electrical engineering major at Penn State University. He started working at Funland in earnest at 14. He said joining the family business was too good an offer to turn down. As a Penn State senior, though, Craig dreaded telling the head of electrical engineering about his joining his family's business instead of interviewing with major companies the way his classmates did. His fears that the head of the department would think Craig's four years at Penn State were wasted were unfounded.

"He told me, 'First of all, if you were going into the electrical engineering profession, you'd probably be going into an entry-level job and would probably work for people you don't know or don't like, or both, and you'd be the low person on the totem pole,'" Craig said. "I asked him, 'What about the education part?' He said, 'We trained you to be an engineer. We trained you to solve problems. You are going to be surprised at what you use.'

"And he was so right. Looking back on it all these years later, the things I've used from my education … when I came into the business, vacuum tubes were giving way to transistors, which were giving way to integrated circuits, and I was in all that, and microcomputers and then personal computers. That was the age I came into the business, and I was able to ride that wave for a while. My job has not always been perfect, and there are times when I wonder 'Why do I do this?' but they don't last very long. There is no question this has been a great job."

Craig's younger brother, Neil, developed a love for amusement park games at an early age. When he was 5, he worked a little ball-throw game at Willow Mill Park, where you had to knock targets with images of cats off the shelf. Neil would crawl up on the bottom board that held the ball return tarp and step on the first shelf to put the targets on the top shelf.

"I never gave doing anything else but joining the family business much thought," Neil said. "I was literally standing on milk crates spinning cotton candy when I wasn't big enough to reach the other side of the cotton candy spinner, so it was always in my blood."

◆ ◆ ◆ ◆

The same could be said about scouting. Al, Craig and Neil are all Eagle Scouts, and Al was scoutmaster of Hershey Boy Scout Troop 203 for 20 years and is still involved with it. In the summer of 1968, Al took both sons and other scouts from his troop to Philmont Scout Ranch in New Mexico, which is considered the Boy Scout's premier "high adventure" base. Philmont features 220 square miles of

Al (front row, center) led a contingent of scouts from Hershey Troop 203 to Philmont Scout Ranch in 1968, which included Craig (front row, second from right) and Neil (front row, far left).

rugged wilderness, the perfect place for multi-day backpacking trips, among other things.

Neil maintained his love of scouting, attending several world scout jamborees, and served on the staff at national jamborees. These all took place during the summer, but Neil said leaving Funland for these events was never an issue.

"I did not miss a scouting event I wanted to attend because of my parents telling me I had to work at Funland," Neil said. "That wasn't paramount. It wasn't that I missed out on much working at Funland; it was probably as much or more fun staying around Funland. We are very fortunate to have gotten to do so much with our family."

Al's feelings about the benefits of scouting had an impact during the many years he managed Funland's personnel. In addition to Al and his two sons, family members Ian Curry, Randy and Gwen Curry's son, and Gail and Bill Henschke's son Mark, both earned Eagle Scout honors as members of Hershey Troop 203. Al believes scouting builds character, and that those few scouts who reach the level of Eagle – according to the Boy Scouts of America, only 4 percent of Boy Scouts attain that rank – are good people to have around.

"I met Al for the first time during my initial interview in the summer of 1989. I was 18 years old, and it was my first real job interview; so, needless to say, I was a bit nervous," remembers David Wilbourn, who worked at Funland from 1989 through 1992. "I took a seat in the office, and after exchanging introductions and a few pleasantries, I noticed he was wearing a Philmont Boy Scout Ranch belt. I saw this as an excellent icebreaker and pointed out that I, too, had been to Philmont as a Boy Scout and that I was an Eagle Scout. Without hesitating, Al extended his hand to me, shook it and asked when I could start. I'd like to think Al's reaction was a reflection on my character – and to an extent it was – but I believe it's more of a testament to his own and to those he has hired over the years. The Boy Scout law states that a Scout is trustworthy, loyal, helpful, friendly, courteous, kind, obedient, cheerful, thrifty, brave, clean and reverent. I truly believe Funland has had the longevity and success it has because Al lives his life by these simple principles and looks to his youthful employees to do the same."

◆ ◆ ◆ ◆

Bill Henschke said he learned early on that Al and Don expected everyone to work as a team to get the job done. If you finish your project, go and help those who are still working. There were no job titles, no eight-hour days or 40-hour weeks, and Al and Don were setting the example. He said his reaction to something totally unexpected that happened his first summer made him think it might be his last.

"We were painting the old Paratrooper, and the ride framework was three feet off the ground," Bill said. "So Al hopped up on that and when he jumped down, his foot landed in a gallon of red paint that we were painting the ride with. He had his foot stuck in it, and he was hopping all over the place. He was mad. And I held it as long as I could possibly hold it, and I burst out laughing. And I thought my Funland career was over at that point. It was hilarious. Paint was everywhere. He decided to keep me on."

Lisa Ginder, upon joining the family business in 1986, was searching for a way to make her mark. She found that in helping Neil with the prizes.

"I was looking for my own niche when I joined the business. Neil was doing most of the stocking of prizes at our games, and I thought I could help him," Lisa said. "So I started doing that, and I would go to trade shows with him. We like to give out a lot of prizes. Some parks offer giant prizes but have few winners. We like to make sure that people get to win something of quality, and it is especially fun to see when the kids are better at the games than adults and win the prizes. I will always remember the smiles on the kids' faces."

When Amy and Steve Hendricks came on in 1990, Steve took over the personnel duties from Al. Those duties included managing about 100 workers in 1990 – a number that grew to 125 in 2018 – and creating work schedules for all the employees every day. This meant making sure all the rides and games were properly staffed while providing the summer crew with some variety and taking into consideration what rides or games they could work, the level of responsibility needed, their individual strengths and weaknesses, and much more. Additionally, everything could change at a moment's notice if what was expected to be a nice beach day turned cloudy, and people decided to come to Funland in the afternoon instead of going to the beach. That meant possibly opening rides that were closed and having to close rides because of the weather, so as personnel manager, Steve needed to be prepared for any and all contingencies.

That, though, all paled in comparison to following in the footsteps of Al, who had manned the personnel job since coming to Funland full time in 1968. In sports, they say the hardest coaching jobs are when you follow a legend – like basketball coach Dean Smith at the University of North Carolina or football coach Paul "Bear" Bryant at the University of Alabama – because so much is expected of you. Steve found that to be true to some degree.

"I was taking over from a dynasty, and the other family members took Al's decisions more readily than those of a newcomer like me, so that was a little challenging," Steve said. "My having worked at Funland for two summers in the mid-1970s did help with my transition to joining the family business. Al was instrumental in teaching us the importance of having a good work ethic, which he displayed on a daily basis, and that there is something satisfying about working hard. He also taught me when you do something, do it right. I can remember doing morning cleanup – one morning each week, the summer employees worked for an hour, usually between 9 and 10 am, cleaning something in the park. My favorite morning cleanup job was cleaning the glass on the pinball machines – and if you didn't do it right, he told you about it, but in a good way. I carried those life lessons around with me, so when I joined the business as an adult, I knew what the philosophy was in terms of working hard, how we were expected to treat customers and that we were all expected to pitch in when others needed help. So in that way, coming on board was pretty easy."

◆ ◆ ◆ ◆

Brad Ginder's brother, Todd, who worked at Funland for more than five summers in high school and college, was a high school industrial arts teacher looking for a summer job. He and his wife, Elisabeth, worked at Funland in the summer of 1992 on a no-strings-attached basis and have been part of the family business ever since.

Todd Ginder working on the Sea Dragon.

"It was one of those opportunities that just presented itself," Todd said. "Because of my background in industrial arts, I was familiar with machines and mechanical stuff and that kind of thing. I thought this was a great way to get involved, a little at a time, three months during the season, and I wasn't really committed to anything. I remember the Fasnacht family welcoming me with open arms. They knew my work experience from my working there as a kid, and we knew the family really well since we all grew up in Hershey."

Todd was also a member of Al's Boy Scout troop. Ironically, he and his family now live, during the summers, in the house he and his fellow Boy Scouts used to stay in when Al would bring the Scouts to Rehoboth. Speaking of family, Todd and Elisabeth have three children, the oldest of whom, Nathan, does information technology work for Funland as part of the fourth generation.

◆ ◆ ◆ ◆

Ian Curry, another member of the fourth generation, took a very different path to joining the family business. He met his wife, Fiona, at Funland, as she came with several friends from her home in Scotland to work at the park for a few summers, the first of which was 2002. One thing led to another, and the summer of 2005 was Ian's first away from Funland, as he moved to Scotland to be with Fiona. They got married in Scotland in 2007, and their first child, Jay, was born in Scotland in 2010. By that point, they had decided to join the family business, and they worked to get Fiona a green card to allow them to do so.

"Joining the family business and keeping it going is very important to me, and my wife is very supportive of that," Ian said. "I can remember clear as anything my mom and dad telling me joining the business is not something I had to do. The pressure I felt was subconscious and my own pressure. I'm the oldest of Don's grandchildren, and I'm proud of what my family has built, and I want to keep it going.

"In this day and age, it says a lot to be a part of something that means so much to so many people. It's not about making money; it's about people having fun, building community and seeing people come back year after year. To me, it says how much we care. I want to keep Funland a family-owned business, and as the third generation gets older, it is going to be up to us in the fourth generation to do that. It is a big challenge, and it is what motivates and excites me every day."

MY FUNLAND STORY:
Sam Cooper, Mayor of Rehoboth Beach from 1990-2017

It's hard to stress how important I think Funland is, because there is no other business in Rehoboth that fully fills the niche of providing affordable fun for the whole family, and especially younger kids, that they do. Over the years, they have had to modernize some to keep up with the times, but they've also been mindful of their past. They still have several rides there that I rode on as a kid. I would think it would be easy to dump those for something that is more profitable.

Sam Cooper

I'm impressed with their family structure. How many families can stay so cohesive? Too many families want to take theirs and run. They are obviously very close-knit, which I think is to be admired in today's world.

The only issue I had, which was early on in my tenure, was that there was a lady on Brooklyn Avenue who complained about the noise. This was related to the pirate ship [Sea Dragon]; people are up in the air, so the sound just goes from there, and that's part of the enjoyment of the ride. I think they tried to be respectful of their neighbors, but they also had a business to run. [Funland did voluntarily agree to close the Sea Dragon at 11 pm on weeknights after receiving this complaint.]

As mayor, I was always cognizant of the fact Rehoboth has become very popular, but I never wanted it to become a place so expensive the average guy was excluded. I think it's great that a young family who can't afford some of the high-end offerings can go to Funland with $5 and give their kids a good time.

CHAPTER 10:
Funland's Games –
Everything You Want to Know

*"The games are a huge part of the Funland experience. I love that they
are on the boardwalk; it's such a classic summer experience with the games,
the lights and the excitement on one side and the beautiful ocean on the other.
My children love playing the games because many of them have prizes
just for playing. None of the games are too challenging or feel like they're
designed to fleece people – they're fair and fun and reasonably priced."*
– Tracy Rose, who visits Funland from her home near Buffalo, New York

Derby, the horse racing game, has crowds three and four deep on most summer nights.

When approaching Funland from the north end of the boardwalk on any
summer night, you will come upon the chaos, excitement and sheer fun of
the Derby, or horse race, game.

It's easy to tell which game is Derby; it's the one with people waiting three
and four deep to play. The Fasnacht family purchased the Derby game in
1982, and it instantly became Funland's most popular game, so much so that
the parts literally wore out and Funland is now on its second Derby game.
Funland also purchased a second Derby-style race game, called Flushing
Meadows, in which people are racing to an outhouse, in 2007.

"Derby was one of our best decisions and investments," said Neil Fasnacht. "I would hate to think how many times those horses have run around the earth since 1982. That's been our bread-and-butter game."

Derby is one of Funland's 17 amusement games, which also include long-time favorites Skee-Ball, Whac-a-Mole, Goblet Toss and Frog Bog. The latter may be the most fun game to watch, as you place a rubber frog on a catapult, hit the catapult release with a mallet and your frog flies into the air. You win when your frog lands on a lily pad. From my years working and watching this game, kids seem to enjoy making their frog fly just as much, if not more, than winning a prize.

Neil said his philosophy is to give out lots of quality prizes, especially to kids, without people having to spend a lot of money.

"The games are all about having winners. When people see you can win – our group games have a winner every time, and we've added more of the winner-every-time games – that attracts others to play," Neil said. "We gear the games more for a younger crowd. We have very few high-level skill games. The idea is that a 3 year old can throw a ring and have almost as good a chance as an adult throwing a ring on a Coke bottle. Same with the Goblet Toss.

"As for pricing, with the group games like Derby and Whac-a-Mole, I'm adamant about keeping them at $1. To me, on a slow afternoon, if a father walks up to Whac-a-Mole with three kids, there's something about $1 that just feels right. If you're doubling that, it would cost that father $8 to play. At some other places, it is $3 to play the group games, and I've seen as high as $5. If we did that, during a full game at Whac-a-Mole, which would be 13 players, you would have 12 people lose $5 in a matter of 15 seconds. That's not the way we want to treat our customers."

It should be noted that both Derby (1982) and Whac-a-Mole (1983) start-ed as 50-cent games, so the price for each has increased just 50 cents over the last 36 years.

◆ ◆ ◆ ◆

Everyone seems to have a favorite game, and a family story that goes along with it.

"Our family's favorite game is the horse races [Derby]," said Chad Ham-merly, who has been coming to Funland since 1994. "We love the fact we could all play together. Our family is so large we'd fill up all 12 spots. It didn't matter who won because we all just had fun playing together. My family and I love the fact that 20 years later, the horse races are still only $1. The kids would stockpile the prizes and trade up at the end for the jumbo prizes. The challenge for the parents was to figure out how to get them all home."

"One of my sons, on his second try on the game with the Wiffle Balls and the goblets [Goblet Toss], he ends up with the grand prize," said Katie Laing, whose sons Alexander and Russell are third-generation Funland kids. "He happened to toss the Wiffle Ball in the goblet in the middle. I didn't see it; I was talking to the game operator, and the next thing I know my son is having a coronary. Oh my gosh. And then, of course, we had to walk around with this gigantic seal for the next hour. He was so excited."

"My youngest son, Logan, is a big fan of Skee-Ball," said Clint Davis, whose two sons do odd jobs around the house all year to earn money to spend at Funland. "One day my older son Evan and my wife split off from our group and Logan and I were hanging out together. Logan got really excited when he saw if you scored at least 250 points on Skee-Ball, you could win a stuffed latte cup. He told me he wanted to win it for his mom, a renowned coffee enthusiast. Logan spent several of his own dollars attempting to win the prize, without success.

"When he got to his 10th dollar I told him this is the last one. He got a serious look on his face but did not say a word. He proceeded to score 260 points and won the latte. He screamed at the top of his lungs as if he had hit the lottery. When we finally caught up with my wife later that night, Logan gave her the stuffed latte. My wife loved it, of course, and asked him how long it took him to win it. Logan said, 'A long time, but you are worth it.' I believe my wife still has that stuffed latte to this day."

◆ ◆ ◆ ◆

Skee-Ball is a classic amusement park game. Funland has had Skee-Ball since it opened in 1962. It started at 5 cents a game, went to 10 cents a game and moved to its current 25 cents a game in 1984, at which point it added prizes for people reaching scores of 250 and higher. It is fun watching Funland's 12

Skee-Ball attracts players of all ages.

Skee-Ball lanes to see the many different methods people of all ages use. The two most common styles are banking the ball off the side and rolling it straight. Like with Derby, most nice summer nights will find all the lanes full from 7 to 11 pm, with many entire families playing side by side.

Funland Game History			
Game	Years	Game	Years
Skee-Ball	1962-Present	Muffin Pan Mania	1988-Present
Splat-the-Cat	1964-70; 1994-98	Ball Falls	1990-93
Spin Paint	1964-81	Knock Down Boom Ball	1990-92
Raceway	1966-67	Mini Skee-Toss	1991-92
Apple Darts	1968-82	Sidewinder	1991-92
Shooting Waters	1968-81	Ring-a-Coke	1993-Present
Tic-Tac-Toe	1971-86; 1991-92	Ping Pong	1993-98
Cork Gun	1971-72	Basketball	1995-06
Ring Fling	1972-73; 1988-90	Caterpillar	1994-Present
Glass Topper	1981-87	Duck Pond	1994-Present
Speed Pitch	1981-84	Skatterball	1998-Present
Goblet Toss	1982-Present	Hi-Striker	1999-2016
Derby (Horse Race)	1982-Present	Beach Ball Blast	1999-Present
Boom Ball	1983-92	Squeeze Play	2005-06
Whac-a-Mole	1983-Present	Flushing Meadows	2007-Present
Tin Can Alley	1984-86	Dog Pounder	2008-Present
Bowler Rollers	1985-88	Super Shot (Long-Range Basketball Shot)	2009-Present
Frog Bog	1985-Present	Water Race	2009-Present
Hoop Shot	1987-92; 2007-Present	Balloon Bust	2014-Present
Flipper	1987-2004		

"It's what people who come to the beach look forward to doing because they've done it every year they've vacationed here," said Neil, who has rolled Skee-Ball "perfect games" of 450 – all nine balls in the 50-point ring – in seven or eight states. "People have their favorite pizza, French fries and ice cream, and when it comes to our games, they have their favorites there, too. Games like the Derby horse race, Skee-Ball, Whac-a-Mole and Frog Bog. We have families that come in and they have a mini-tournament among themselves. At Skee-Ball, people who don't hit that really high score will keep grinding away, and they'll hit a couple of smalls and then they hit a medium, and you can see them building up their piles and getting ready to trade up to the next level."

Laing, whose son won the grand prize at Goblet Toss, is such a Skee-Ball player. She will only use one specific lane, as she feels it gives her an edge.

"I've learned how to bank the ball of the sides. There is a scuff mark on the machine at the far right next to the wall and nearest the ocean, and I know exactly what to aim for," Laing said. "I can't hit the hundred, but I can hit the 40 and 50 and be sure to win, and my kids think it is great; they will sit there and collect the stuffed animals while I play."

◆ ◆ ◆ ◆

Selecting prizes for all the games is one of Neil's hardest jobs. Imagine doing this for 17 different games, many of which allow you to trade up to win bigger prizes, so you may have as many as five or six different levels of prizes, such as small, medium, large, extra-large, giant and choice. For example, the size of a small prize is often something you can easily hold in your hands, while the choice prize may be a stuffed animal as much as five-feet tall or wide. The others cover all ranges in between. Some games, like Super Shot, a long-distance basketball shooting game, and the Derby horse

Neil is always on the lookout for good prizes.

race game, have game-specific prizes – basketballs and horses, respectively – but Neil factors in many things, including the age of people who play a certain game and what items those people would be interested in winning. Ideally, they would also be prizes that have a shelf life of more than one summer.

The vast majority of prizes Funland awards are soft-stuffed animals – soft-stuffed as opposed to hard-stuffed to make it easier for families to fit them in the car for the ride home – most of which are manufactured in China. To provide a sense of scale, Neil estimates they award more than 300,000 stuffed animals every summer, and tens of thousands of balls. He purchases containers on a cargo ship to bring them to the United States. Shipping cost is a key consideration. Neil said if the soft-stuffed animal is below a certain size that justifies it taking up the space you pay on ocean freight, those items come as finished goods. For those really big giant and choice prizes, such as the largest horses at Derby, which may be 48- or 60-inches high, the outer skins are shipped from China, and they are stuffed domestically.

Then there is the lead time necessary to get the prizes to Funland. Neil said for the items coming from China, you need to purchase them 150 to 180 days before you are able to use them. He purchases most of that summer's prizes the previous November on the trade show floor at the International Association of Amusement Parks and Attractions annual conference, where he works with 10-12 different prize vendors/manufacturers.

"I go to the trade shows and talk to other people in the industry to find out what's working, but a lot of it is a crapshoot," Neil said about the prize-selection process. "It's guesswork in trying to figure out what's going to be the next hottest item and what's going to hit during the season. Generally, you're much better going with prizes from a Nickelodeon-type, continually-running show that's strong with kids year after year, like SpongeBob SquarePants, whereas some movies are more of a flash in the pan. This year [Neil said prior to the start of the 2018 season] I'm going big with sloths, like in the Geico commercials, and hamsters. Even the colors I choose can make a big difference on how popular an item is. And if an item becomes big, say, in June, and I didn't order it in November, there's no way I can get any for that season."

So what have been the most popular Funland prizes of all time?

"The single strongest piece among all age groups may have been the California Raisins. Kids liked them, and grandmothers did, too," Neil said. "SpongeBob, Pokemon, Trolls and Minions have all done very well. The single hottest piece we ever had, though, was Bart Simpson. It was small by comparison and had a molded head. When I first saw it, I remember thinking, '$13.50 for that thing?' I was allocated only 60 a week. Literally they were like gold. I would drive up to exit 8A off the New Jersey Turnpike on Friday night, my night off, to pick them up and bring them back. I put them in the Muffin Pan Mania game. The kids didn't want to work the game because people were bugging them to buy them."

◆ ◆ ◆ ◆

The biggest challenge Neil faces every year is not prize selection, but storage space. "My whole job in the spring boils down to two words – create space," he said.

Funland stores prizes literally in every space it can find, most of which are within the park's perimeter. There is underground storage – with more than seven feet of head room – from below the office at the back of the park behind the Jungle of Fun all the way up to the far end of the Merry-Go-Round, and it's as wide as the two rows of kiddie rides. High above the park, what's referred to as the second floor, there is storage – with 10 feet of head room – from the office all the way to the boardwalk above the row of kiddie rides closest to Delaware Avenue. This includes what used to be the dormitory above the front of the park where I and many summer employees lived when working at Funland. All told, there is about 10,000 square feet of storage space, almost all of which is used for prizes.

"We try to bring a lot of our prizes in early, in April and May, and that's always to our advantage," Neil said. "We can't bring them all in at the same time, though, as we'd have no place to store everything. For example, I divide the number of Derby horse prizes into three shipments spread out to arrive at different points during the summer so I have room for them. In the height of the season, we are going through a tractor-trailer load of prizes every three to four days, basically two a week in July and August. We have 17 games, and at every one of those group games when you hear a bell ending the game, a prize is being handed out. We'll go through over 1,000 basketballs at Super Shot in a week.

"My best day of the summer is when I hit my last really big load of prizes coming in, and I have the space to handle it. At that point, we have a lot more going out as prizes than is coming in for the rest of the summer. That usually happens at some point in July."

While Funland customers see few signs of the volume of prizes coming in, except for the aforementioned tractor-trailer shipments, the daily prize replenishing is much more on public display.

"For people who are around in the mornings, it's interesting to have them see what we do in terms of restocking from a busy night the night before," Neil said. "I'm up in the drop on the second floor, and people are texting me their orders and I'm throwing stuff down, and from up there, it looks like little ants running to all their games and getting them ready for another day."

To Neil, the joy of his job is measured in smiles, and in occasionally going above and beyond to create an experience kids – and their parents – will never forget.

"Seeing the little kids' faces when they win never gets old," Neil said. "One time, my wife, daughter – who was about 5 at the time – and I were at a restaurant, and you could tell the group beside us was celebrating another little girl's birthday. And when she blew out the candles, someone said, 'What did you wish for?' And she

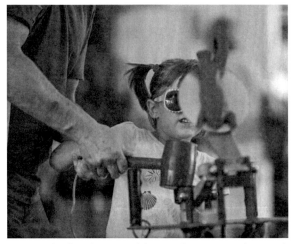

Frog Bog has long been one of the most fun games to play – and watch – as people attempt to catapult a rubber frog onto a lilly pad.

said she wished she'd win the biggest prize at Funland. So we actually waited for them on the boardwalk until they came up, and when we saw them, we said, 'We can make your wish come true. What would you like?' It is little things like that that stick with you."

MY FUNLAND STORY: Allison Dodds, as Told by Her Mom, Kathy

Everyone at Funland knows my daughter, Allison, who we call Alli. She has autism and does not speak at all but communicates well in other ways. We come to Funland every weekend, from the opening weekend in May to the closing in September. All the workers either know Alli or get to know her, and they accept her, respect her and, I believe, enjoy her.

Alli was adopted from Guatemala. We got her when she was nine months old, and she only weighed six pounds. She has had a difficult life. At Funland, though, she is like a different person. It's her special place, a place that brings her great joy and where she can be herself.

Allison (Alli) Dodds

She loves the rides, especially the Himalaya. Last summer we were in Rehoboth for five weeks, and we came almost every night. Alli even made her first real friend at Funland several years ago, and that really helped her to come out and to feel accepted for who she is. There's just something about Funland that brings out the best in Alli.

Going to Funland is like coming home. The workers are among the nicest young men and women you can find anywhere, and the way they treat Alli is amazing. I believe they are treated with respect by the family that owns Funland, whom I love. Each one is kind, friendly, dedicated and demonstrates a work ethic that is rare these days.

Allison is the No. 1 fan of Funland, and the way the workers and family treat her just makes me smile when I think about it. Funland is the best!

CHAPTER 11:
The Making of the Haunted Mansion

"It is the holy grail of dark rides. I have probably walked, ridden and photographed about 300 different dark rides, but there's been nothing created that is so unique, so one-of-a-kind, so magical and timeless. The Funland Haunted Mansion is as good now as it was back then, and that is amazing. The ride is my No. 1 dark ride of all time. The presentation just blows your socks away. It is incredible."

– Dark ride expert Bret Malone

Funland's Haunted Mansion is ranked among the world's best dark rides.

One thing Funland lacked in its early years was a signature ride, the sort of ride people go on again and again, one they wait patiently in long lines to ride, and that created a sense of anticipation that would seemingly always be exceeded in a slightly different way each time.

Signature rides tend to be very large, like roller coasters, take up a lot of space and are not something you can experience elsewhere. Funland's signature ride would need to be different by necessity. Its footprint is very small – smaller than many big-city blocks. It had limited resources in the early years, and almost all of its rides were purchased from major ride manufacturers and could be found at amusement parks and traveling carnivals alike.

Add to the mix the ride the Fasnachts had in mind – a Haunted Mansion, which was one they had never operated, had no experience with, and wanted to build themselves and make first class with limited funds. They had what one might optimistically call a challenge.

It gets more interesting: The Fasnacht family wanted to build the ride primarily over the Bumper Cars. At the time they were working on the Haunted Mansion in the late 1970s, there were less than a handful of other dark rides – the industry term for haunted or spooky rides – that had the track overhead rather than on the ground, and none of them had to go up 18 to 20 feet with turns. There was some debate about whether it could be done at all.

"When we decided we wanted to use two levels for our ride, we had to try to figure out how to get people up and down," Al said. "When we built the ride, most of the dark rides had tracks on the floor and were only on one level. We had to come up with some sort of a braking system to guarantee the cars did not come down too fast."

The Fasnacht family heard about a ride manufacturer in Greer, South Carolina – Gerald "Jerry" Barber – whose company, Venture Rides, had built a portable dark ride on a flatbed trailer. The ride took people from the ground to a height of about 4 feet. Funland ride's transportation system would need to take people almost five times higher.

Barber never had any doubts he could make this work. A physics and chemistry major in college, Barber is best known as an inventor. He has more than 50 U.S. patents; his most famous is for the "Free Fall" ride that is a staple of most major amusement parks, including Funland, under a variety of names. Venture Rides was the second-largest ride company in the country at one point during its 18 years of operation in the 1970s and 1980s. He and his son,

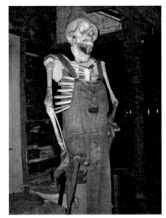

Todd, co-invented "The Reef Ball," an artificial coral reef that has won numerous awards for being environmentally friendly. His latest company, Barber Wind Turbines, takes technology from the amusement park industry – his patented wind turbine design borrows from and in some ways resembles a Ferris wheel.

"We knew we'd have no trouble getting to the second floor, but we didn't realize initially the steep incline in such a short distance; it was almost as steep as an elevator," Barber said. "The problem is, you've got to get traction. So what happened is the wheels that pull the cars

The fire-fighting skeleton douses the imaginary flames.

up the hill wanted to slip. So we added an extra wheel, which caused it to squeeze down hard on the track, and that worked. Coming down, it was very hard to control the downhill speed, especially if it got a little bit wet or damp, which you have around the ocean all the time. The track we built for them was designed for not-so-steep inclines and declines, and we tried to modify it as best we could."

After Venture built the track, it was set up and tested, successfully, at Venture's facility. The Fasnacht family decided the track should be galvanized – a process of applying a protective coating of zinc to steel or iron to prevent rusting – to shield the track from the effects of the salt-air environment Funland calls home. But the heat of the galvanizing process caused a slight warpage and buildup of material on the ends of the track where they connect together. So when the track was shipped to Funland, nothing fit together.

To say this was a big problem is an understatement. The whole ride depended on the track being able to support the weight of the cars and to transport people safely up to the second story and back down to the first floor at the end of the ride. The track had to be right. The question was, what adjustments needed to be made to the track to get it that way?

"The whole track system was based on having a 2-inch pipe, and a smaller pipe that was supposed to slide in, and then you welded it together," said Al's brother Don, the person in charge of ride maintenance for most of Funland's existence. "Well, the pieces did not fit. Venture galvanized it, which we wanted, but we had to grind all that down to get it to fit. I adapted an old pipe threader that we had and took the pipe thread part and ground them down like a metal lathe, and then we would grind each one off with the pipe threader so it would slide inside the other tubing. It was just crazy, and it took a lot of time."

Randy Curry said Don's creativity in solving the vexing track issues is something he will never forget.

"Don came up with an ingenious way to make those two pieces of track fit together with the tools we had to work with at the time," Curry said. "He basically said, 'This is what I'm go-

ing to do, because this is what I have in hand.' He used another device, which was pretty much a tap-and-die set that you use for pipe threads; it's a long arm with a cutter that goes over-top the pipe, and he had to modify the cutter. Instead of having to make it cut threads, he made it so it was cutting the galvanizing off the outside of one of the connector pieces. We had 500 feet of track, and each piece of track might have been 6 feet long, so you start to add up the multiples of that times two … his ability to look at that and see the whole picture and figure out a way to make it work really stood out in my mind."

◆ ◆ ◆ ◆

The Haunted Mansion project began in September 1978, and the goal was to have the ride up and running for the start of the 1979 season. The track issues added several months to the timeline, as the ride would not be ready to open until late in the summer of 1979. At the same time they were working on the track, Al was looking for some expertise to design the ride, and he had a clear vision in mind.

"We wanted this to be a family ride," Al said. "We didn't want it to be strictly a teenage ride where you had people jumping out with a chainsaw and that kind of thing. We knew it was not going to be easy to put something together that would be entertaining, scary enough for a great many of the people and yet not so scary that you couldn't take your 6 year old on it."

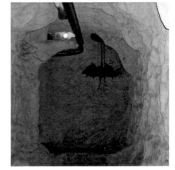

The bat cave is one of the ride's many cool features.

Al reached out to Jim Melonic, who was making a name for himself designing and creating dark rides. A professionally-trained artist, Melonic also knew how to draft, draw, build and fabricate, all useful skills when it comes to creating a haunted mansion. He worked as a set painter for legendary dark ride creator, artist and designer Bill Tracy, who built many dark rides from 1960 until his death in 1975, including several by the name of Whacky Shacks. He also built three dark rides in Ocean City, Maryland, as well as dark rides at Pennsylvania parks Knoebels in Elysburg, Kennywood Park just outside Pittsburgh and Dorney Park in Allentown, according to The Bill Tracy Project. Melonic said he is still inspired by Tracy's work, and ironically, in 1977, he came to own Tracy's old company, but gave it a new name: Fantasies and Dreams. He started his work at Funland with that company, but completed it as JMM Studios, which his company still goes by today.

At Funland, his scope of work included everything from painting to putting together the animation and tricks, building the sets and, in general, making the dark ride a truly memorable experience for young and old alike. Melonic and Al sat down and sketched out what would happen in the Haunted Mansion room by room, after which Melonic would create the sets.

"I did the signs for the front of the ride, did the masonry on the chimney, did the paintings over the fireplace, the wallpaper, the organ, the breakaway wall with the bookcases, the shaft, the catacombs down under, the graveyard scene, the spider, and did the truck trick, where the truck's headlights and horn go on," Melonic said. "The overhead track and car system really helped with the design, as you can't tell where you are going unless you are looking up. When I set the tricks, I set them to draw people away from where the tricks were. So if I had something going to jump out on the right, I would draw them to the left purposely so that it would scare them and make the ride more interesting."

◆ ◆ ◆ ◆

One of the ride's unique features is going outside to provide a view of the boardwalk and ocean.

Another unique feature is there are two points where you are taken outside, in a sense. Near the start, after you climb to the second story, you have a view of the Crazy Dazys and Gravitron before you enter the living room, and later in the ride, you can see the boardwalk and ocean for a few seconds before the ride reenters the darkness. These are just a few of the special traits that make the ride memorable.

"All the major theme parks have some sort of haunted house ride, but the Funland ride is truly special," Malone, the dark ride expert, said. "For someone who has never ridden Funland's Haunted Mansion, I guarantee you that it will scare the crap out of them. It still does. The room with the organ player, the crashing through the bookcase, the misdirection on the outside where you crash through the wall, just those little touches keep you on guard the whole ride. It's just timeless."

As the Haunted Mansion was nearing completion, the Fasnacht family wanted to have a permanent fence to form the queue or wait line that would be fitting for a dark ride. The family decided a wrought iron fence might work. They saw an advertisement for one in the Philadelphia area, and Al and his wife, Jean, hopped in their pickup truck and went to check it out.

"The fence that was advertised had spikes, and wasn't what we had in mind," Al said. "I then asked the owner if he knew where we could get some ribbon, or rounded-top, fencing. He said he did, and to follow him to another neighborhood. The fence he showed us was on a corner property and was just what we had in mind. So I paid him several hundred dollars, and I began to uproot the fence. All of a sudden the man had vanished and I said to Jean, 'What if that guy just sold us someone else's fence?' I didn't wait for an answer … I loaded that pickup as fast as I could, and we hightailed it out of the City of Brotherly Love."

◆ ◆ ◆ ◆

Funland's Haunted Mansion opened to rave reviews and long lines, which is still the case all these years later. It is widely considered one of the best dark rides anywhere according to experts like Malone and the Dark Attraction and Funhouse Enthusiasts (DAFE), an organization  dedicated to documenting and supporting dark rides and fun houses. DAFE did a member survey each year from 2002 through 2011, and Funland was always in the top 10 of members' favorite dark rides from across the U.S., having ranked as high as No. 2 in 2007. Others on this list included dark rides from Disneyland, Walt Disney World and Universal Studios, to name a few. Heady company.

"The thing that makes Funland special is the Haunted Mansion," said DAFE board member Alan Stromer. "I know a lot of dark ride enthusiasts, not just in DAFE, and there is not one person I know who has gone through Funland's ride and said they didn't like it."

Adds fellow DAFE board member Joel Styer: "Many dark rides have some dull spots, but there is always something happening in Funland's Haunted Mansion. That ride keeps your interest, and you want to ride it over and over. It's all about the experience, and they do a great job of making sure every single trick is working. The ride really is a production, which explains why people are willing to wait in such long lines night after night to ride it. It is just a fun ride."

◆ ◆ ◆ ◆

One big question, from a customer perspective, was the scariness factor. Would young kids be too scared to ride? Would older kids not be scared enough? And, perhaps most importantly, would people who have ridden the ride several times no longer be scared at all? Based on the constantly long lines from the time the ride opens, as well as the comments of many people who have experienced the ride, it seems to strike an almost perfect balance. People seem to find something new or different about the ride each time they board one of the all-black cars to begin the ascent to the second story.

Al says one of his favorite jobs in the park is to unload the Haunted Mansion cars after the ride, as you get to witness all kinds of reactions the second people exit the Mansion. Many people also share comments about the ride, especially those kids who had been debating whether or not they were old enough to ride, who now want to do nothing more than get back in line and ride again.

Funland began selling photos of people in the cars taken during a scary part of the ride as a keepsake of the Haunted Mansion experience. For Clint Davis and his family, these photos have taken on a life of their own.

"In 2013, my parents announced they were starting a new family tradition of renting a beach house in Broadkill Beach – just a few miles north of Rehoboth – each summer," said Davis, who lives in Roanoke, Virginia. "We went to Funland one night and rode on a couple of rides when my brother asked my kids, who were 9 and 6 at the time, if they would join him on the Haunted Mansion. They had been on the version at Walt

Wendy Davis and her son Logan react while on the Haunted Mansion.

Disney World, but were not ready for what laid inside Funland's version.

"They came out half-terrified and half-thrilled. After that night the

Haunted Mansion became a family tradition for us; I would purchase the best 'Scared Photo' taken at a certain point in the ride. As the years went by, the photos got more and more creative, including one year when my boys memorized where the photo is taken in the ride and gave the picture a thumbs up. Funland has become such an annual cornerstone in our lives; a place where we have many great past memories, with many more to come."

MY FUNLAND STORY: Brian Allen, Owner, Flyland Designs

Illustrator and graphic designer Brian Allen is best known for creating the Philadelphia Flyers' mascot, Gritty, which debuted at the start of the 2018 National Hockey League season. He was just as excited, though, about two projects he did for Funland — a graphic wrap for the park's simulation ride (Sim Rider) and a mural for the upslope of the Haunted Mansion — because of his lifelong connection with the park. Allen, 36, talks about those experiences and what makes Funland so special to him and his family. To see more of Allen's work, check out his portfolio: www.flylanddesigns.com.

My grandparents — both on my father and mother's side — have lived in Rehoboth for decades. In fact, it's where my parents met. I've been visiting Rehoboth several times a year since I was born. It's great to see my own kids as excited about Funland as my brothers and I were. And since many of the classic rides are still in great shape — like the Fire Engines — I have photos of my kids enjoying the same rides I did decades ago.

Working on the mural in the Haunted Mansion was a once-in-a-lifetime experience and quite an honor, as the ride was one of my favorites as a kid. The plan was to paint the upslope so it looked like an old hallway, and use black-light paint

Brian Allen with his artwork inside the Haunted Mansion.

to make the creatures stand out. Because of the slope, using a ladder wasn't always possible, so that was tricky at times.

The biggest challenge, though, was the black-light paint process itself. Ever try painting in the dark? In order to really see what the effect of the paint would be, I often had to paint in the dark, lit only by a black light that I moved around from place to place. I was constantly tripping over things and knocking things over.

I only had a week to complete the painting, so I made sure to plan out the mural first on the computer. I used printed sketches with a grid on them to help me redraw the images onto the wall. I'll admit there were some evenings when I would be the only one in the whole park still working, and it got a little creepy in there!

It feels wonderful to know that I put a little mark on something that will be enjoyed by so many for countless years to come, including me and my family. What makes Funland so special is its timeless feel. It seems like no matter what stage of my life I'm in, Funland is a place I can go back to that stays frozen in time.

Allen painted the Haunted Mansion upslope in just one week.

Working with the Funland family was wonderful. Everyone I worked with still says hi to this day when I take my kids there. They even invited my family to ride the rides with the Funland families when no one else was in the park. That was a day we will never forget!

CHAPTER 12:

The Day Funland Closed During the Summer

*"It is amazing to me that our closing
Funland for one day would be national news."*
– Al Fasnacht

*Jean Fasnacht (far right) with husband Al and kids (from left to right) Neil, Gail and Craig, in the
1960s.*

Al met Jean Walmer in kindergarten; they shared the same homeroom
every year through 12th grade and went to Hershey Junior College together
for two years. Al went on to Penn State University to finish his degree in
accounting, and they got married the summer between his junior and senior
year. They did practically everything together. They were both avid golfers,
Philadelphia Phillies fans and very much family oriented. They had three
children, Gail, Craig and Neil, got into the amusement park business, first at
Willow Mill Park and then at Funland, and each made a lasting impression.

While Al ran Funland, managed the personnel and kept the books, Jean managed the dorms where the summer crew lived, helped in other ways around the park and was the primary caregiver for their kids. Living in Rehoboth in the summer and Hershey the rest of the year, the family was pretty much always together.

I got to know Jean well in my six summers as a Funland employee. She would plan our meals, do most of the shopping and worked a lot in the office. She was like our mother away from home for the summer and tried to make sure the summer crew had everything it needed. Housing and feeding 26 people was a big undertaking, and she played a large role in creating the family atmosphere that made working at Funland so unique.

◆ ◆ ◆ ◆

So when Al's lifelong partner and matriarch of Funland passed away on August 11, 2013, the Fasnacht family talked about how best to honor her life and pay their respects. The most popular idea was to close Funland for a day to have the funeral in their off-season home of Hershey.

This was not as simple a decision as it sounds. Funland had never closed for a day during the summer season between Memorial Day and Labor Day for a non-weather-related event, and there were some mixed feelings about turning people away.

"When my mom died, we talked about what we were going to do," Craig said. "We decided we would close Funland for a day so we could all go to the funeral. My dad said, 'No way.' It had nothing to do with our losing revenue. He said, 'What are the people going to do who are here for vacation?' He was thinking about the customers and was worried about people having something to do. We really had to lean on him pretty hard and say, 'Al, we're closing Funland, and you are coming with us and we're going home for the funeral.'"

Says Al: "I had a disagreement with most of the family, who felt we should come home and close the park. I felt we had an obligation to the people here who were on vacation. I had a lot of people acknowledge that shutting down for a day was the right thing to do, so it worked out well."

The family decided Jean's funeral would be on Tuesday, August 20 at the First United Methodist Church of Hershey, Al and Jean's church for more than 60 years. The story of Funland's closing literally became national news, appearing in USA Today, as well as in newspapers in Washington D.C., Baltimore, Philadelphia, Pittsburgh and many other towns in the Mid-Atlantic region with people who vacation in Rehoboth. The USA Today article read as follows:

DELAWARE Rehoboth Beach: Funland will go dark today for the funeral of co-founder Jean Fasnacht, who died Aug. 11 at 84. Fasnacht and her husband, Al, opened the popular amusement park in 1962.

Wanting to give people advance notice, the family posted signs on Funland's large green garage-style doors facing the boardwalk about the impending closure:

Due to a death in the family
FUNLAND
will be closed on
Tuesday, August 20
We will reopen at our regular
operating hours on Wednesday the 21st
THANK YOU for YOUR
UNDERSTANDING

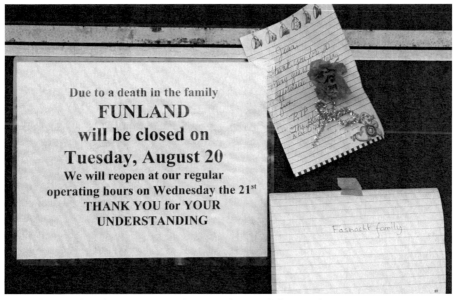

Funland's green doors became a memorial to Jean when people learned of her passing.

Those green doors became an impromptu memorial to Jean, as people brought notes, cards, flowers, a wreath and more to express their sympathy for the family that has given so much to Rehoboth Beach residents and visitors alike for the last 50 years. It was a moving sight, and further recognition of the impact Funland and its owners have had on millions of people who have visited the park.

The funeral featured eulogies from Craig and Neil. It was a fitting tribute for a life well-lived, a life that revolved around her family, including a husband she had known since she was 5. "When we eulogized our mother, Neil and

I both thanked our father for choosing so well," Craig said. "And we could have said the same thing to mom."

Among the many guests were former and present Funland employees. "I worked at Funland the summer when Al's wife passed away, and even though he had to watch that happen, he still made an effort to get to know every single new employee and keep in contact with the returning employees," said Sarah Yeager, who worked at Funland from 2011 through 2015. "I attended the funeral and saw some other former employees, and when Al saw us, he started tearing up because he was so happy that people would make the trip to support him and his family. I also think it shows what kind of a boss he and the rest of his family are. If former employees are willing to travel, and some of them pretty far, to support him, it speaks to the kind of impression he left on their lives."

> 47
>
> Dear Fasnacht family,
>
> We were not privileged enough to know Jean or any member of your family, but we do know how much joy you have brought to our family for generations — from my mom who first went to Funland as a teenager when you opened, to my youngest who at 7 is just brave enough to ride the Superflip ... 5 times in a row! We are thinking of you in this time of sorrow, and hope that Jean's legacy lives on in many more generations. Rehoboth wouldn't be Rehoboth without Funland!
>
> With thanks,
>
> The Taubert + Friberg families
> New York / Charleston, SC

One of many cards and letters the Fasnacht family received after Jean's passing.

Even the funeral procession to the church rekindled special memories from an earlier time. "Jean worked for my grandfather at the Hershey Dairies when she was young," said Carl Maurer, who worked at Funland from 1986 through 1990. "When she passed, the funeral procession went by the spot where the old dairy building stood. Back at the church after the service, Al asked me if I noticed that. I was proud to say I did."

◆ ◆ ◆ ◆

While Al agreed to go home for his wife's funeral, he made it clear that if he passes away during the summer, his wishes are they honor him by keeping Funland open. The odds of that happening are somewhere between slim and none.

"My dad is adamant that we will not close Funland if he goes in the summertime, and no one is going to sign a pledge in blood on that," Neil said. "He's always been about the customer and guest, and how do you explain to a 3 or 4 year old that Funland is not opening its doors in August? His philosophy from Day 1 has been that if people are vacationing here for the week, he'd like to see them in Funland every night, because they don't feel like they are being taken advantage of and are getting safe and affordable entertainment for the whole family."

MY FUNLAND STORY: Tracy Rose

Amusement parks are a staple of summer to me. My parents bought season passes to a park near us, in Buffalo, New York, when I was 6 years old. They have continued the tradition, giving passes to myself, and now my daughters, as Christmas presents, 32 years and counting. The happiness I feel watching my children light up as they take a spin on a ride or win one of the games must be the same feeling my parents felt. It's such an integral part of who we are, and I love that I carry on a tradition.

My daughters, Ariana and Isabella, were 4 and just under 2 when we first discovered Funland. It was one of the

Ariana and Isabella Rose at Funland.

reasons I wanted to visit the Delaware coast from our home near Buffalo. I expected it to be a fun, yet expensive, afternoon at a tourist trap, but I absolutely loved it and couldn't wait to take the girls back again later in the week. Since that trip, we have spent four summer vacations in Delaware. Funland is the highlight for my daughters.

Funland feels like heading to a place where time stands still. The sights, sounds, smells and tastes you encounter at Funland would be hard to place in any given era. There's a feeling of an almost tangible nostalgia there – it's a place where time doesn't interfere. It reminds you of carefree childhood happiness. I wish I could bottle that feeling! There's something so perfect about its location, on the boardwalk, beside the ocean, that contributes to the magic of Funland.

When we discuss visiting other places, the children don't want any part of the conversation. Funland remains the highlight of their summer, so every year we return to try to capture that feeling of carefree childhood happiness again.

CHAPTER 13:

All About Al

"Al is an institution. He and his family have provided affordable family fun to millions of people over almost 60 years, and he is a role model for what a business owner in a town like Rehoboth should be. Al has very high standards about always doing things the right way, and he's always been happy and very supportive of our success. He is just a super person."
– Nick Caggiano, owner of Nicola's Pizza

Al and his family have given Funland customers many reasons to smile since 1962.

I've known Al Fasnacht since the late 1970s and have talked to more than 100 people about him and his family in working on this book. Common words and phrases used to describe him include: leader by example, family man, honest, giving, principled, stubborn, competitive, caring, fun-loving, practical joker, hard worker, compassionate, thrifty, athletic, role model, disciplinarian, team player, mentor, friendly, responsible, authoritative, determined, teacher, good businessman, loyal, helpful, kind, cheerful, supportive, trust-worthy and courteous.

Two things that have always stood out about Al to me are his leadership style and work ethic, which in Al's case are so intertwined and similar that it can be hard to find examples of one and not the other. He is a leader by example, someone much more interested in demonstrating what he expects than simply telling you. So whether it is picking up trash in the park – something I learned from Al and still do to this day – or going to help other family members after the job he's been working on is completed, he knows it is one thing to say it and another to do it. He addresses problems right away and head on, making it very clear what he thinks, but also not losing sight of the teaching opportunity, and he's not one to hold grudges. As for his work ethic, how many 90-year-old people do you know who work five hours (and often more) a day from late May through early September, lift 40-pound bags of garbage as part of a daily trash detail while working the kiddie rides for two hours every night during the season?

"There is nobody to this day who works harder than him," Neil says about his dad. "He embarrasses you in the winter; he will be out there in 32-degree weather scraping paint off a ride at 87 or 88. It's like I always joke: I hope I work that hard when I am his age, but I don't work that hard now, so I'll have to step up my game to get to that level."

Adds Fiona Curry, who started at Funland as a summer employee from Scotland in 2002 and who, along with her husband, Ian, are part of the fourth generation and joined the family business in 2011: "I remember when I first started working at Funland, I heard stories about how hard Al worked, and that he never took a break. Recently he swept the entire sidewalk on both sides of Brooklyn Avenue [which borders Funland to the south], and it just looked immaculate. I could sweep that sidewalk and it would not look anything like that. He gives that little extra – he took a dustpan and brush out so it looked absolutely perfect. I remember thinking that when I sweep this someday, I'm going to make sure I take the dustpan and brush out and get that last little bit of dirt. It looked so amazing when he finished."

◆ ◆ ◆ ◆

Al's first job was selling newspapers after school outside the Hershey chocolate factory at age 9, and he has been working ever since. He went on to deliver papers before going to Milton Hershey's truck patch, where they grew and sold fruits and vegetables. He would pick strawberries and other fruit and do orchard work as well as weeding. He then moved to the greenhouse, where he worked in high school and the two years he attended

Hershey Junior College before going to Penn State.

In addition to work, Al's high school years included scouting – he went on to become an Eagle Scout – and he played three sports at Hershey High School. He intended to play golf (a lifelong golfer, Al has three holes in one; interestingly, all with a four iron), football and basketball – both his parents played basketball when they were younger – until an upperclassman "encouraged" him to switch from basketball to wrestling.

"In ninth grade, I went out for the junior varsity basketball team," Al said. "All the winter sports athletes dressed in the same locker room. So as I was getting dressed I see this older student walking towards me. When he got to me he said five words: 'Kid, what do you weigh?' I hesitated and told him about 90 pounds. He said, 'Come with me. We need a 95-pound wrestler.' That didn't do anything for me. I had never seen a wrestling match.

"So then he said five more words: 'You will earn your letter.' Well, in those days, earning your letter, that was IT. I had visions of these seniors with their dark blue sweaters with the bright orange H on it, so I went to wrestling practice. That's how I got to be a wrestler."

That older wrestler's name was Ted Lenker. He was a senior during Al's freshman year (1943), and Lenker enlisted in the Navy after graduation. Al said he was always sorry he never thanked Lenker for introducing him to wrestling. After Lenker passed away in 2012, Al reached out to Lenker's wife, Mildred, to share the story about her husband's role in Al's wrestling career.

Al went on to win four varsity letters in wrestling and finished second in the state finals at 138 pounds as a senior in 1946, a feat his brother Don equaled in the same weight class three years later. Al also earned three varsity letters in both football and golf, and was inducted into the Hershey High School Athletic Hall of Fame in 2017. Hershey Junior College did not offer wrestling at the time – Al would later help start a wrestling program there – so he continued wrestling through the local YMCA and was the Middle Atlantic Amateur Athletic Union champion in his first year of junior college.

Al, 2-2 in his Penn State career, has been involved in wrestling for more than 60 years.

Hershey Junior College offered just two sports at the time – basketball and golf. In 1946, when only eight people attended the first basketball practice, Al was recruited, and became a two-year starting guard. Al said his aggressiveness had teammates joking that he was "scoring more takedowns on the basketball court than the wrestling mat."

He continued his wrestling career at Penn State, where he went 2-2 during the 1948-49 season that was cut short due to a shoulder injury. In what would be his last match, he took on highly regarded Joseph Settanni of Syracuse, although Al did not learn how good Settanni was until after he completed the 6-5 upset victory.

"While we were warming up for the match they introduced us and let everybody know how good he was," Al said of his opponent, who to that point had not lost a dual meet in his college career. "If I heard that, I probably would not have wrestled well. But I was able to beat him, and as I was walking off the mat, my teammates and coach were going crazy. I could not figure out what was going on until someone finally told me. You win some and you lose some!"

Al continued his wrestling career as an official and was considered one of the best in the country when he retired after 15 years of working high school and college matches. From 1957 to 1971, Al officiated 468 dual meets and 76 tournaments, including two NCAA Division I and six NCAA Division III tournaments. Being chosen to officiate NCAA tournaments is a prestigious honor, and a clear indication of how he was perceived by those in the college wrestling community.

"To be selected to officiate at the NCAA Division I wrestling champion-ship means you are the cream of the crop as an official, one of the top 25 or so in the country," said John Hosage, a former college wrestling official. "Al was the kind of official I wanted to be as I was working my way up the ranks. He was honest, consistent and confident, and he controlled the meet. You did not fool with him, but he was a real gentleman at the same time. You could see the respect the coaches and wrestlers had for him. He was one of the best."

After retiring as an official, Al served as a volunteer assistant wrestling coach at Lebanon Valley College in Annville, Pennsylvania, about eight miles northeast of Hershey, where he got to coach his son, Neil. "I could always hear his voice no matter how loud the gym was, telling me what to do," Neil remembers. Al continued his support of wrestling at both the state and national level and is a member of both the Pennsylvania Wrestling Hall of Fame and the National Wrestling Hall of Fame for his more than 60 years of service to the sport.

Al did not stop wrestling after college. One time he was playing basketball with a group of men from his church, and Al, at 5-foot-9 and 135 pounds, was guarding Bill, who was 6-foot-4 and 240 pounds. Things got rough, the two ended up in a wrestling match, and Al pinned him. That, as it turned out, was the first of their two bouts.

"He and I both played tennis, but we would not play with the same group," Al said. "Then one time Bill was playing in the same group I was in, but I didn't know it. So he found out I was there, sneaked up on me, threw his racket down and grabbed me from the back. And so I reversed him and pinned him again. He didn't like that and couldn't accept the fact that a 240-pounder could be handled by a 135-pounder. I told him, 'Bill, if you'd put on a few pounds you would be dangerous.'"

◆ ◆ ◆ ◆

Like wrestling, Al has been involved with scouting for more than half a century. Al served as scoutmaster of Hershey's Boy Scout Troop 203 for 20 years, where he placed an emphasis on outings, adventures and athletics. He would announce an upcoming camping or hiking trip, would tell everyone where to meet and would take anyone who showed up, pretty much regardless of the weather.

"One time we planned a winter campout and were going to leave Friday night. It started snowing early in the day, but by the time we were going to leave it was really coming down," Al said. "I got a call from one of the mothers, who said, 'Al, I told Todd there is no way you're going camping with all this snow.' And I said, 'What did Todd say?' He said, 'You don't know Al.' We went on the trip."

Al continues the story, after mentioning that while his older son, Craig, was old enough to be in the troop, younger son Neil wasn't, but he brought him along anyway. "So we're parked up on a hill and walking down the lane to the cabin and the snow is piling up pretty good, and Neil is in the back of the line. And you can hardly see him. He falls over, and I look back and I can't see him. I said 'Neil.' And he said 'Yeah.' I said 'Get up and get moving.'"

Having fun was a big part of scouting for Al. He liked to play practical jokes, which included raising fellow scoutmasters' underwear up the flagpole. The scouts themselves were not immune.

"One time I was sleeping in a little too long for his taste, and we were on a campout, and he knocked the whole tent down around me," said Ned Zechman, who became an Eagle Scout and who worked at Willow Mill Park for Al and his family. "I still have the picture just as the tent fell down, and I was struggling to get out with the sleeping bag partially around me, and they put the flag up, so I was standing there saluting the flag, and Al was smiling."

Zechman, who retired in 2011 after spending 35 years as a hospital administrator, the last 16 as president and CEO of Children's National Medical Center in Washington D.C., said he implemented several leadership lessons he learned from Al that benefited his career.

"Al set such a tremendous example for everyone, and that's something I took forward: appreciating everyone in every position," Zechman said. "We had a lot of housekeeping staff and dietary staff, and we had high-paid heart surgeons. Treating everyone the same and trying to set the example for everyone, and not being too big to stop and pick up paper on the floor and things like that, are lessons he taught me. If you walked by paper at the park and did not pick it up, you were in a lot of trouble."

◆ ◆ ◆ ◆

Al's most elaborate practical joke involved a friend from Hershey named Tom Davis, a person running for office in South Carolina by the same name, and the stealing of a campaign sign. The sign said, "Elect Tom Davis," who was running for lieutenant governor. Al and his wife, Jean, were on vacation in Hilton Head, South Carolina, with friends from Hershey, Dick and Nancy Zimmerman, who were also friends of the Tom Davis from Hershey, who is a retired plastic surgeon. Al said they passed the sign almost every day of their vacation, and he and Dick quickly hatched a plan.

"After seeing this sign, Dick and I looked at each other and said, 'We've got to take that sign home,'" Al said. "The sign was right along the main drive into Hilton Head, three lanes of traffic each way, and here we are dismantling this sign. I thought, 'Wouldn't it be funny if we got hauled in for stealing the sign?' Here was Dick, the CEO of Hershey Foods, one of the top Fortune 500 companies, and he gets jailed for theft?' Fortunately, we got the sign home without any problems."

The Tom Davis from Hershey held two Christmas parties at his house on consecutive nights each year, and the plan was to put the sign up in his front yard – the sign just said "Elect Tom Davis" without the office – right before the first party so people would see the sign and ask Tom what he was running for. The plan worked to perfection, as guests starting quizzing Davis about his political ambitions.

"All during the party there was this buzz about the sign, and I had no clue," Davis said. "It was a fun joke, and I loved it because Al and Dick were sort of my heroes, and it was something they went out of their way to do for me. I kept the sign up for a few days, and when I took it down, I had it in my garage for a long time.

"An interesting side note: I asked people to bring food to the party for the Hershey Food Bank, which they would place in a grocery cart on my front porch. The day after my second Christmas party, Al and his family would pick up all the food that was collected and take it to the food bank. It seemed like every time there's something good in Hershey, you find a Fasnacht."

◆ ◆ ◆ ◆

Another cause Al got involved with was visiting prison inmates, known as prison ministry. A friend of his brother Don, Ken Ernst, was found guilty of murdering his son in 1973. The Ernst family vacationed in Rehoboth, and they would come into Funland. A friend of Al's, Bill Long, who was a good friend of Ken's, mentioned to Al some years later that he was going to visit Ken in prison.

Al asked Bill to let him know the next time he was going, as he might like to go along. Al thinks his first visit with Ken was in the early 1980s, and he has been visiting inmates, mostly those in for life, since that time at five Pennsylvania prisons: Coal Township; Rockview, in Bellefonte; Camp Hill; Houtzdale; and Huntingdon.

Al said he, Bill Long and Dottie Bell visit inmates every two or three weeks when he is not at Funland. He gets new inmates to visit largely through word-of-mouth referrals; inmates will tell other inmates about Al. If they are interested in having Al visit them, the inmate will let Al know.

"A good many of the inmates I visit have been completely cut off from their families, and they are very happy to have company," Al said. "Many of the people I visit have been in prison for two-thirds of their lives. I think knowing that challenges me to be able to do things that can help other people. It is one of those situations where you get more than you give. It is a real eye-opener. I know that when we come out of prison I feel good about having been there."

Occasionally the people Al visits do get released. Chris Nolen is one example. Nolen was found guilty of murder and went to prison at age 16. Al had been visiting Nolen for 20 years when Nolen was released in February 2017. He met Nolen when he was at Rockview visiting Ernst. Nolen said his time with Al made a huge difference.

"Prison is a dark place; I've seen many guys die in prison because they did not have any support system, but Al was there for me," Nolen said. "He's not afraid to open his life up to people. Through his help, things have changed around for me. To have someone like Al there, not giving a handout but a hand up, has been powerful. He truly cares about people. When I got released, he was right there to help out and took me to a very nice dinner. He is a true believer."

Nolen introduced Al to Anthony Curry, a fellow inmate and friend at Rockview. Al had been visiting Curry for a number of years when Curry told him he would be released in July 2017. Al told Curry he'd like to pick him up and drive him home to Chester, Pennsylvania, if possible. It turns out Curry was to be released on July 3, right in the middle of one of Funland's biggest weekends. Al and his son Neil went to Rockview anyway to take Curry home.

"I was interested to see what the actual release from prison was like," Al said. "It was just like he was walking out with us after a visit. The guard said to him, 'I don't want to see you back here,' but that was about it. Anthony did not do a hop, skip or jump, he did not raise his hands, he was just very calm. I've talked to him recently [February of 2018], and he's driving trucks and seems to be doing well, which I am glad to hear."

Randall (Randy) Eugene Dietz, an inmate at Coal Township who was convicted of first-degree murder in 1987, started visiting with Al around 2005. Dietz said the two talk about all sorts of things, including current events, sports, Funland, family and friends, personal life experiences, their faith and much more. It is clear from Dietz's correspondence with me – all in the form of letters – that he knows a lot about Funland, to the point where he is giving me suggestions of good stories to include.

In Dietz's letters, he shares the kind of stories I've heard about Al from many others, making me forget for the moment he is an inmate in a state prison. He talks about Al's generosity, compassion, friendship, natural instinct to help others and mentoring with enthusiasm. He says Al's visits provide a much-needed escape from his everyday life.

"Al's visits mean enough to me that I'm willing to get strip-searched before and after each visit, which I refused after a couple of visits from some-one from the prison society," Dietz said. "When I had aspirations of writing children's books, Al sent one to me as a guide and for inspiration. At Christmastime, he sends me some money, which allows me to purchase phone time, music and games, and commissary items. At one point I read three articles about the International Children's Surgical Foundation (ICSF), which performs free surgeries for children with cleft lips and cleft palates in developing countries. I decided I wanted to contribute, but I didn't have ICSF's mailing address, so I asked Al to get it. Not only did he do that, but he and his family's foundation donate annually to ICSF.

"I'm not as surprised that Al has seen me as long as he has as I am amazed he comes to visit me and other inmates at all," Dietz said. "His visits mean I am loved. They also make me behave, so I don't lose my visiting privileges. Al loves people, and it's nice to see him interact with others when he visits me, especially the kids. It's never anything big, but it's him being nice to others.

"One time a lady half his age dropped some change at the vending machines – where Al buys me lunch so I don't have to eat the prison food – and Al was down on his hands and knees right away retrieving the change for her. What impressed me was the speed at which he did it. Not only has Al become somewhat of a family member and mentor to me, but also a friend and excellent example of how a person should live."

❖ ❖ ❖

Al (second from left) was one of four people inducted into the Junior Achievement of Delaware Business Leaders Hall of Fame in 2016.

Al's good friend Dick Zimmerman, his co-conspirator in the Tom Davis sign gag and the former president and CEO of Hershey Foods, once said that if he were starting a business, he would want Al to run it. Others have taken notice of his business and management acumen, including the Junior Achievement of Delaware Business Leaders Hall of Fame, which honored and inducted Al in 2016. He was one of the first 60 people to receive this distinction.

Part of Al's appeal is being a people person. He gets to know Funland customers – especially the parents and grandparents of young children – while working the kiddie rides, while always keeping his eyes on the ride. He's quick with a joke and a smile, and is very approachable, as evidenced by the many customers who talk to him each night. He's also quick to compliment parents for their child's thoughtfulness.

"Occasionally I will get a little one who will thank me for helping them get into a car or unbuckling their safety belt," Al said. "They say, 'Thank You' not because their parent is looking over their shoulder and saying 'What do you say?' They do it because it is part of their routine. And when I get an opportunity after that happens, I pull the parent aside and say, 'Your little one just thanked me for helping her off the ride. You're doing something right. Keep up the good work.' Parents really appreciate that. It not only builds goodwill from our standpoint, but it lets them know their child is appreciative."

Al is known for his random acts of kindness – delivering Hershey's chocolate to people at Christmastime, putting a Hershey's kiss on the ride operator's seat for the employee coming back after their evening break and much more. To him, it's all about making others happy, something he and his family have mastered at Funland, and elsewhere, leaving an indelible impression on those they have come into contact with.

"Dick [Zimmerman] and Allen were in Rotary together in Hershey, and on the way home they would stop at McDonald's because Dick loved McDonald's milkshakes," said Dick's wife, Nancy. "So when Dick was too sick to attend Rotary any longer [he passed away in June 2014], on Monday after Rotary Allen would stop by our house with a McDonald's milkshake for Dick. He is a thoughtful, thoughtful, kind person."

That thoughtfulness extends to Funland's current and former summer employees as well. Al is the one who has always said, "You're not working for us, you're working with us," and that relationship does not end when your Funland career is over. Al has attended many former employees' weddings, funerals of employees and their family members and other important life events, and you get the sense he is honored to be there.

Al and his son Craig came to my dad's memorial service in 2014, which meant a lot to me. He had gotten to know my dad well over the years, and that relationship was the reason I eventually worked at Funland.

Neil remembers one weekend where he accompanied his dad to the wedding of a former Funland employee on a Saturday and then drove the next day to see the Eagle Scout ceremony of a son of one of Funland's first female employees. To Al, it is simply the right thing to do.

◆ ◆ ◆ ◆

Another telling sign of the impact Al has had on Funland employees over the last half century is the number who come back during the summer to visit him. In most cases, he greets them by name, regardless of how long ago they worked at Funland or how many years it had been since he last saw them.

Rarely a day goes by that former employees don't come back to see Al, pictured here with Ben Fishburne and Conor Cusick.

"I always thought it was amazing that with all the kids he worked with year in and year out, he always remembered something unique about them, like the school I was from and that I wrestled, let alone all of their names," said Duane Kenney, who worked at Funland the summers of 1992 and 1993. "Even more impressive is I will sometimes stop by the office when I bring my family to the park to say hi, and Al still remembers me and when I was there, quickly finding the team pictures of the summers I was there on the office wall. He nails it every time."

Adds David Hughes, who worked at Funland the summers of 1980 through 1985, and in 1988: "I live in the Midwest, and I don't get back to Funland as much as I would like. But each and every time I go, Al always recognizes me and calls me by my name no matter how many years had passed since my last visit. He always makes me feel like I am seeing family."

◆ ◆ ◆ ◆

One word I've never heard used to describe Al is quitter. If he starts something, he finishes it, and does so in a way that meets his perfectionist standards. Perhaps the toughest part of aging for Al is realizing he may not be able to do the same things he did 40 and 50 years ago, a battle in which he is unwilling to admit defeat.

His daughter, Gail, says there are times when she and her siblings want their dad to not do something, and that they sort of draw straws to decide who is going to talk to him, as they know he does not want to hear what they have to say.

In September 2017, some members of the Fasnacht family participated in a hike to raise money for Lou Gehrig's disease, or amyotrophic lateral sclerosis (ALS). The father of Chris Darr, Funland's current personnel manager, had ALS, and Al planned to walk two miles on the Rehoboth Beach boardwalk to raise money in honor of John. (John passed away in February of 2019.)

"I had a knee that had been bothering me, but I wanted to be a part of it for John's sake, and when we finished, Gail said to me, 'How's the knee?' I said that it was bloated. She said, 'Why didn't you quit?' I said, 'You know me for how many years? You know I never quit. I don't know what that word means.'"

◆ ◆ ◆

Part of Al's secret is he never acts his age. His friends from Hershey think he's crazy to continue going to Funland for the summer and working as hard as he does. For Al, there is nothing he'd rather do more. In the early days of Funland, he was the oldest person playing in intense football games that were touch in name only on the beach directly in front of Funland. The games pitted the Fasnacht family against its summer crew and would quickly draw many spectators to watch the action. Softball games were equally competitive. Work hard, play hard and keep doing the things you want to do, no matter how surprising they may be.

"For many years at the International Association of Amusement Parks and Attractions (IAAPA) trade show, I would get together with the Fasnachts, and at the end of the day, we'd usually hang out by the pool," Alan Kanter recalled. "And in 2015, Al was there, he said, for the last time. So we are sitting there, talking, and all of a sudden Al is gone. When he came back a few minutes later, we asked him where he went. 'I had to go down the waterslide.' So here he is, at 87, going down the waterslide because it is fun."

Working at Funland is fun for Al, and probably never more so than in recent years. Part of that may be because he never expected to live this long. Al suffered a heart attack at 51, and had bypass surgery and has a pacemaker, none of which have slowed him down at all.

"When I was in my 30s and 40s, my mom would tell me that if I didn't slow down I would have a heart attack before I was 50. She was wrong," Al said with a smile. "But to still be able to do things like work at Funland at my age, I am way ahead of the game, that's for sure."

The doctor who was on call when Al came to the emergency room with chest pains was Maurice Lewis, who would serve as Al's doctor for the next 35 years. He said Al was a good patient, and an even better person and friend.

"Al knew what he had to do after his heart attack, and he did it; a lot of people don't. They just get lazy and let it go, but he's stayed very active," said Lewis, who retired in 2015. "He doesn't want anything. He just wants to give, and he's happy doing it. He's like an angel. There are not many people like that, and I've seen a lot of people. He looks you in the eye; he never looks away, and he smiles. And that smile warms your whole body. He's just the best."

◆ ◆ ◆ ◆

Each summer I worked at Funland, I was very excited at the beginning but was ready to return to school by the time late August rolled around. The same is true with the Fasnacht family, with one notable exception.

"In earlier years, I was like everyone else in the family; 'thank goodness the summer is over,'" Al said. "Now, at this point in my life, when it is time to close up for the season, I have the thought in the back of my mind that 'this could be your last year, Al.' So the sense of relief is not what it used to be."

Al has been working the kiddie rides for a few hours each night for more than 40 years, and has no plans of stopping.

It's hard to believe any person can be more deeply involved and committed to a business's success than Al is to Funland's. His passion is on display every night while operating the kiddie rides, and the fact that he was born before the Stock Market Crash of 1929 adds to his charm. His code on the walkie-talkie system family members use to communicate with each other is "28," for his birth year (1928). Some would say with age comes wisdom; others say the older you are the more stubborn or unwilling to change you may be. In Al's case, it is probably a little bit of both, with a lot of gratitude thrown in for good measure.

"I count my blessings that I am still able to work. I can't tell you how many times in recent summers people have said to me, 'Oh, glad to see you are still here.' And then they add, 'How long are you going to keep doing it?' My stock answer is, 'Until they carry me out.'"

MY FUNLAND STORY: Aubrey Eppes

This is an excerpt of Aubrey's introduction of Al Fasnacht when he was inducted into the Junior Achievement of Delaware Business Leaders Hall of Fame in 2016. Aubrey, who was in third grade at the time of the induction, is the daughter of Junior Achievement of Delaware President Rob Eppes.

Tonight, I have the privilege of introducing our Hall of Fame inductee, whose business literally changed my life. The first time I ever played Skee-Ball with my mom and dad was at Funland. And we love Skee-Ball. The first time I ever went boating was at Funland. The first time I ever went up in a hot air balloon, an airplane and a helicopter, it was at Funland.

And just this past summer, I got to go on a behind-the-scenes tour during a Junior Achievement job shadow event at Funland, learning how the business works and all the jobs they have there, for young and old alike.

It was on this job shadow that I overcame some of my biggest fears and finally went through the Funland Haunted House.

Ladies and gentlemen, one of my heroes, Allen Fasnacht.

Aubrey Eppes with Al.

CHAPTER 14:
Giving Back

*One of the greatest things in life is the opportunity to do
something for someone else, and the satisfaction you feel as a result.
The earlier in life we learn that, the happier we will be."*
— Al Fasnacht

*Sussex Academy is one of 25-30 groups Funland provides discounted or free tickets
to each summer.*

Doing nice things for others is a way of life for the Fasnacht family. If
Funland had a mission statement, this would be at or near the top. Examples
of this include the low ticket and game prices, the quality of prizes – mostly
stuffed animals – it gives out, and having a closing time determined by the
customers.

Other examples are less obvious but no less meaningful. A former Rehoboth mayor talks about how the Fasnacht family would help longtime Rehoboth residents in need. The family created the Fasnacht Family Foundation in 1999, which has given more than $500,000 in support of charities in Rehoboth and Hershey, as well as to national and international organizations; it opens the park to special-needs kids and provides discounted tickets to 25-30 kids' groups that could not otherwise afford to come; and it supports important Rehoboth events and activities that benefit all Rehoboth merchants and visitors. Al "retired" in 1990 when another family joined the business so there would be more money available to pay them; and the Fasnacht family takes stuffed animals home and donates them to a variety of worthy causes, including at a Christmas party for the Four Diamonds Fund benefiting kids with cancer at the Penn State Hershey Medical Center, which they have done for the last 25 years.

"Every mayor, in most communities, has a short list of merchants that can be counted on just about any time the community needs help, and Funland and the Fasnachts were on my list," says former Rehoboth mayor John Hughes. "You get an old Rehoboth resident, end of their years who has fallen through the welfare net, and as mayor you call on your merchants sometimes and dig in your own pocket. When I needed help for someone, they were among the first people I called. They are salt of the earth and among the best in Rehoboth. Most of the merchants we think the world of, but I think there was an extra degree of community spirit and care at Funland."

◆ ◆ ◆ ◆

Speaking of community spirit, I will never forget the time in my first summer of Funland when Al asked me to help a group of special-needs kids who would be coming to the park when it was normally closed to ride the rides. As I would later learn, this was not a one-time thing, and the experience had a profound impact on me and my coworkers, one of whom that day was Doug Reeder.

"I remember Al's philosophy of giving back to the community," said Reeder, who worked at Funland the summers of 1978 through 1982. "Every now and then before the park was open, Al and the family would invite special-needs kids from the area to enjoy the rides. He would ask several of us to assist with the children, getting them on and off the rides, and even in some cases riding with them. The joy on their faces was something I will never forget."

One such group of special-needs students is from the Howard T. Ennis School in Georgetown, Delaware. The Ennis School provides educational services to students with significant disabilities from preschool through age 21. Buddy Snyder, a special education teacher at the school, has taken a group of older students between the ages of 18 to 21 to Funland the last six years. The Fasnacht family hosts the Ennis students for about two hours free of charge, opening up the park just for this group.

"The once a year we take the kids is probably the only time most of them will get to experience something like Funland," Snyder said. "And whether it's the first time or the third time going to Funland, our kids all have the same reaction. They all light up as soon as we walk into Funland; just seeing the rides and hearing the noises, the smiles are on pretty much every kid's face.

"One of the things that stands out to me is seeing Mr. Al in action at Funland. He's constantly in motion and doing and smiling and interacting. It's amazing to see someone putting that much effort and energy into making others happy. And he refuses to take any money. We've offered to make a donation or pay for the staff's lunch, but he's never charged a dime. He's never asked for anything.

"It makes you realize there are some good people in this world that want to do for others out of the kindness of their heart and are not looking for any recognition or anything in return. It is the feeling of knowing you've made someone's day, or year. The generosity he shows to the kids is beyond amazing. He's one of a kind."

Another school group that visits Funland annually is Sussex Academy, a charter school also based in Georgetown, which is about 21 miles west of Rehoboth. Math teacher Jaime Bahder has taken about 250 sixth- and seventh-grade students to Funland as an end-of-the-school-year celebration for the last four years, at a discounted rate. It's a trip both students and Al look forward to.

"Al literally shows up at school every year to talk to me about our field trip to Funland. He's fantastic," Bahder said. "As for our kids, they know that if they get in trouble between February and April they are not allowed to go to Funland, so starting in February they are on their best behavior so as not to miss the trip."

One of Bahder's recent students, Keena Webb, talked about the Funland trip.

"When I heard we were going to Funland on our field trip, I was ecstatic," Webb said. "All of my childhood memories came flooding back to me at once; screaming when I flew in the air on the Sea Dragon, giggling when I got tossed and turned on the Tea Cups [Crazy Dazy] and dancing around when I won a prize from Skee-Ball. I couldn't believe I would be going with my school friends.

"Once there, we quickly got wrist bands [all-day passes] and climbed aboard the Gravitron.'What songs would you like to hear?' a smiling employee asks us. My friends and I giggle, then we tell him a few of our favorites. We press ourselves up against the mats, while the dome starts to spin. Soon enough, we're stuck to the mats because the ride is spinning so fast. Our favorite music blares in our ears as we flip upside down without falling over. Time flies, and it is soon time to go. It meant so much to me to be able to go to Funland again. It was like a little reunion; not with my friends, but with Funland!"

There was another, smaller trip to Funland for Sussex Academy students that Bahder said the Fasnachts made very memorable.

"A couple years ago we did what we call an expedition, where we mix up all the grade levels and we pick a topic. That year the topic was ghosts and goblins," Bahder said. "So Funland actually brought us in for free and we did a behind-the-scenes tour of the Haunted Mansion. They had five of six people take our group of 30 to 40 kids through, told us how they made everything, the changes they make every year and more. It was amazing."

◆ ◆ ◆ ◆

When Al and Don's mother, Sis, passed away in 1998 at 91, the family used most of her money to redo the Merry-Go-Round, including adding panels to the outside of the ride. What was left was the seed money to start the Fasnacht Family Foundation. Of Al and Don's seven children, five are daughters, and the two sons have no male children, something that factored heavily into the foundation's name.

"We did it because after Don and I are gone, there is no extension of our family. There are no male heirs," Al said. "And we wanted to put in place something that would at least bear the Fasnacht name and carry forth some sort of philosophy of giving that we tried to maintain."

The Foundation donates to charities big and small and local, regional, national and international. The majority of recipients are local, meaning close to Rehoboth or Hershey. There are five officers who decide every year which charities to donate to, and how much to give to each. Those officers are Al, Al's daughter, Gail Henschke, Don's daughters, Gwen Curry and Lee Ann Fasnacht, and Gail's daughter, Erin Darr. None of the officers have ever received any compensation from the Foundation, and the Foundation's expenses are almost nonexistent. There is no advertising, no consultants, no fees paid to anyone. Money is donated to worthy charities, and donations to the Foundation are made exclusively by family.

"The five of us work together to decide where the money goes each year.

It's wonderful," Gwen Curry said. "Just to have the family name there, and to know it was started with my grandparents' estate when they passed. I'm proud that my dad and uncle decided to start this. It is a wonderful legacy for our family."

In 2018, the Fasnacht Family Foundation donated to 63 charities, in donations ranging from $500 to $2,500, and gave a total of $70,000. Several themes emerge in looking at the list of recipients: a focus on helping kids, fighting hunger, providing health services for those who can't afford them, faith-based organizations and more.

◆ ◆ ◆ ◆

Funland was one of Henry's favorite places.

The list of charities remains pretty much the same year after year, with a few being added or removed based on the officers' interests; local, national and international events and ties to the park itself. An example of the latter is the story of how it started contributing to the Hope for Henry Foundation.

In 1995, Laurie Strongin and her husband, Allen Goldberg, had a son, Henry. Within a few weeks of Henry's birth, Strongin and Goldberg learned Henry had Fanconi anemia – a rare, inherited blood disorder that leads to bone marrow failure and often proves fatal. Henry passed away at the age of 7, and Strongin created a nonprofit foundation in Henry's honor called Hope for Henry. She also wrote a moving account of Henry's life called Saving Henry: A Mother's Journey. In the book, she has a chapter about Funland and talks about how it was one of Henry's favorite places. The Fasnacht family heard about this story and connected with Strongin.

"I had a reading at Browseabout Books in Rehoboth when my book came out, and someone from Funland came to the reading," Strongin said. "And the family has been donating money to Hope for Henry ever since my book came out through its foundation. I think that is a really beautiful thing. So Funland is sort of perpetuating Henry's spirit by supporting Hope for Henry.

"We still go to Funland. You know, I actually carry a Funland ticket in my wallet. Always. It's like a little good luck charm."

Another recipient of Fasnacht Family Foundation donations is Someone To Tell It To, a nonprofit organization/ministry started by Central Pennsylvania pastors Michael Gingerich and Tom Kaden, who believe lives can be changed by giving people a safe environment in which to tell their stories to someone who is really listening to them. Gingerich got to know the Fasnacht family well when he served as pastor of the First United Methodist Church of Hershey, where many family members belong, from 1993 to 2003.

Gingerich and Kaden have written two books, the first of which, Someone to Tell it To: Sharing Life's Journey, has a chapter about the Fasnacht family's work ethic and approach to business called "The Road Less Traveled." When asked about this, Gingerich says, "They've just taken a road less traveled in the way they treat people; they are a different kind of business people than what you might often see. It's not just about the profits. It's about the way people are valued and honored."

The Fasnacht Family Foundation has donated to Someone To Tell It To every year since it began in 2012, and the family shows its support in other ways as well. Craig Fasnacht has served on Someone To Tell It To's board, and family members often attend the organization's charity fundraisers. Gingerich said those and other acts of kindness speak to the Fasnacht family's generosity.

"During my first year as pastor at First United Methodist Church, Al and his wife, Jean, invited our family to Rehoboth, and to Funland, to stay in their apartments for a week," Gingerich said. "I have three sons, and our youngest son has severe intellectual disabilities and autism. One of the reasons I think they invited us was because that son just loves the beach and the ocean, and they delighted in having us there and seeing him delight in being there. Our son was calmer, more relaxed and happier in general at the beach, and he could sit there for five or six hours at a time and just be in heaven. We will never forget that. Even after I left the church, up until when Jean died [in 2013], they invited us every year to stay with them."

◆ ◆ ◆ ◆

When Don's youngest daughter, Amy, and her husband, Steve Hendricks, joined the family business in 1990, Al stopped drawing a salary so there would be more money available for family salaries. Al did not tell me this; I learned about it from two family members.

For Al, this was an easy decision. He was 61 at the time and had been working since the age of 9. And while he had no thoughts of truly retiring – he still doesn't – he also did this, in part, to send a message to the younger generations in the family business.

"When Amy and Steve decided to come into the family business, it would have required some adjustment in everyone's income to make way for them," Al said. "I figured that with how much was in my retirement plan that Jean and I would be able to live very comfortably without any pay from Funland, which we have. My feeling is, you are being paid through the years by your company's contribution to your retirement, and when you reach a certain point, you should stop drawing wages and start to live off of that retirement, which is what that is for.

"I've tried to get the third generation to see the benefits we've been able to build up through the retirement program; they are going to be left with more money than they know what to do with. And they are going to spend the rest of their lifetime trying to figure out how to give it away. Because the way things are going, and unless things change drastically, they won't have the need to give it to their kids, as their kids will build things up the same way they have. If I take this full cycle, the sooner other family members stop drawing wages, the more money that's available for salaries for the next generation coming on. It eliminates some of the necessity to increase prices for what we offer at Funland. It's a matter of wanting to give back what has been a gift to you."

◆ ◆ ◆ ◆

Al and the rest of the Fasnacht family have given much to employees — like those pictured in the 2012 team photo — and customers for more than 50 years.

As with other aspects of his life, Al's actions speak louder than his words. In addition to the Fasnacht Family Foundation, Al gives a lot of money each year to charities and causes he believes in. He's made it known to his family he would like to give all his money away while he's living. He has his work cut out for him.

"I once heard a story about a gentleman who was giving to various causes, and his philosophy was that he wants his last check to bounce," Al said. "The inference was that his last check would have been to one of his charities – the unlucky last charity. I would love for that to happen.

"I don't need it, and I've been trying to give it away. Some number of years ago I made the mistake of giving $50 to every charity that called me on the phone or sent me a letter. The next year I started getting requests from charities I've never heard of, and it has been that way ever since. I'm gaining on it, but at the rate I'm going, my last check isn't going to bounce."

Neil said he and his siblings support their dad's approach and are grateful for all their parents, and Funland, have given them.

"We could not have been handed a better opportunity," Neil said. "We're not scraping to get by, and we're not worried about job security. It has been a very good life. It's like the sign we used to have in the office; 'Success is relative. The more success the more relatives.'

"Dad has given us so much. We don't need to say 'Hey, what are you leaving us in your will?' As dad would say, 'Be appreciative of what the good Lord has given you.' We've had a lot of little things where someone has needed something, and they might ask him for a couple thousand dollars. Dad wouldn't question it; he would do it to help someone out."

◆ ◆ ◆ ◆

One of the charities the Fasnacht Family Foundation gives to annually is the Bethesda Mission, a homeless shelter in Harrisburg that's operated since 1914. Prior to the Foundation's contributions, though, Neil came up with a way to help the mission during a time of critical need – between Thanksgiving and New Year's Day – for five years in the mid-1990s.

Neil approached the Fox's grocery store chain, which was based in the Hershey area (and which was acquired by Karns Quality Foods in 2006) with an idea that would help multiple charities and people in need around the holidays. The plan was for the Fasnachts to donate stuffed animals that Fox's would sell at four of its stores, starting the day after Thanksgiving until just after Christmas. All sales proceeds would go to charity, with Fox's and the Fasnachts deciding who would receive the proceeds.

Not only did the Fasnachts donate the stuffed animals, but Neil created the store displays and handled all the restocking at no cost. Neil said that during the five years, the combined total given to charity was around $65,000. The Fasnachts gave its share to the Bethesda Mission.

"I remember being in Hershey and going with Neil to the grocery stores," recalls family friend and amusement park executive Alan Kanter. "He did it solely to raise money for charity. It is all about doing something for someone else. The Fasnachts don't live to want. They want to live. It is just who they are."

MY FUNLAND STORY: Hazel Croner, as Told by Her Son, Charles Croner

Hazel Croner was best known as a fashion illustrator for Glamour, Harper's Bazaar and Vogue magazines, among others, but her real joy was doing on-the-spot portraits, especially of kids, at Funland in Rehoboth Beach. She did that for more than 20 summers, ending in the mid-1980s. She passed away at the age of 98 in 2011.

Mom had a little spot in the back of the park, near the office and next to the Motorcycle ride. She came with her easel and a variety of knickknacks to distract children. I remember numerous times watching her trying to do portraits of kids who were very squirmy, and wondering how she was going to get them to sit still long enough. She would pick up one of the knickknacks in her non-drawing hand, get the child to focus on that for a minute or so, and she'd have her portrait.

Hazel Croner doing a portrait at Funland.

She would take summers off from her job to go to Rehoboth to draw. It was a calling for her. She became very good friends with the Fasnachts, especially Sis, who was Al's mom. The Fasnacht family was so generous and kind to her, and mom felt like she was part of the Fasnachts' extended family.

Doing portraits at Funland was what she looked forward to all year. It was like a dream for mom, in that it allowed her to step out of the rigors and challenges of day-to-day living and go to a place where all you feel is joy. That was Funland to her.

CHAPTER 15:

Funland on National TV

"This is one of my favorite stories of all time.
I love doing stories about ordinary people who do extraordinary things,
and I think they fit that category. The level of happiness at Funland
was something I have never seen before."
– CBS News Correspondent Chip Reid

Al being interviewed by CBS News correspondent Chip Reid.

When CBS News producer Carrie Rabin called Al in the summer of 2015 to talk about CBS doing a story on Funland, he had no idea at the time how big an impact the story would have on the park, his family and the people watching the four-minute-plus piece called "A fun ride back in time."

"When the woman from CBS called from Washington, I assumed the program was a local show, and they wanted to do something on us because a lot of people in Washington D.C., come to Rehoboth," Al said. "I had no idea what the show was. When I found out it was a national program, I just shook my head. It didn't make sense to me why a national show wanted to profile a little park like Funland."

The idea was Rabin's. While visiting Funland earlier that summer with her young daughter, she noticed the old photos throughout the park, and thought how cool, and rare, it was to have a multi-generational business that has been so successful, and was so inexpensive. After doing some research on Funland, she ran the idea by her correspondent, Chip Reid, a Delaware native who spent some weekends as a teenager on the Rehoboth boardwalk, and he liked it as well. It ended up running on the CBS show Sunday Morning, in part because one of the show's senior producers had been to Funland and quickly green-lighted the piece.

Rabin and Reid work out of CBS's Washington bureau, where many stories they cover focus on the White House, the Capitol and politics. So a trip to the Delaware shore to do a piece on a fourth-generation amusement park was something they and their crew looked forward to.

"We do a lot of Washington-based stories, so it was a thrill to spend a night and a morning at such a fun place and watching so many people having fun," Rabin said. "We interview a lot of people and go to a lot of places, and not everyone is as genuine and kind as the family who owns Funland. I got the sense they were not lovely to us because we were from the media; I got the sense they were just lovely people."

The shooting would take place on Friday, and Rabin wanted to start as early as possible, to capture all the behind-the-scenes work the Fasnacht family does to set the park up for the day. Part of that included Al performing his daily trash duties, something that really resonated with viewers. To hear Al tell it, he volunteered for that job to continue pulling his weight in the business.

"I can't tell you how many people come up to me and talk about my taking out the trash," Al said. "I guess they think that guy is a nut, to be doing that at my age, which is why they remember that.

"The CBS show has been great for us. It has had quite an impact on a lot of people, especially those who had

Al says many people ask him about taking out the trash.

never heard of Funland; I guess it has given Funland a face. They know that I'm part of the family that operates it, so they are constantly saying they saw the CBS piece on Funland. Many don't even know what program it was – many think it was on 60 Minutes – but they have seen the show and got a good feeling from it."

◆ ◆ ◆ ◆

It is usually Al the people who've watched the CBS piece – which has also received more than 42,000 views on YouTube – come to see. Rabin said after talking with several family members, it became clear the Fasnachts' elder statesman would be the focal point; his level of caring about and passion for the family business were evident right away.

His family jokes that the national TV coverage has made Al a celebrity. For some time after the CBS story aired, Al was much sought after; people wanted to take photos with him, get his autograph, and, more than anything, share their Funland stories with him.

"He has groupies, ladies in particular, and they come in and say they saw him on television, and he just smiles," Al's oldest son, Craig, said. "But then in his quiet moments he says, 'Who would have believed that dinky little Funland would have ended up on national television?' That's kind of who he is."

Adds longtime family member Bill Henschke: "That CBS clip made a big impression on a lot of people. It really spread the word about Funland, and people visited us from all over the country. Most people came to meet Al and get their picture taken with him; his expression of honesty and love touched a lot of people.

"There was a family from Maine that visited us that summer mainly to see what Funland was all about and to meet Al. They have started vacationing in Rehoboth on an annual basis and make a point of saying hello when they arrive. There are many stories like this; Al has touched a lot of lives over the years."

In true Al fashion, while he's grateful people want to share their stories with him, he's still not sure what all the commotion is about, especially more than three years after the story ran. In fact, he worries sometimes half-jokingly that his star turn from the CBS story impacts his ability to provide the kind of customer service he prides himself on.

"Even now, hardly a night goes by that someone doesn't say to me, 'I saw your television show.' They often add, 'Don't change a thing.' And they often ask if they can take a picture of me with their family," said Al at the end of the summer of 2017. "It gets to the point where I am trying to hustle, and I'm being held up."

◆ ◆ ◆ ◆

Everyone seems to have a favorite part of the CBS piece on Funland. Some like the shots of the young family members of the fifth generation, who are shown "testing" the rides and crushing empty boxes. Others like the historical photos of the park and rides. Al taking out the trash gets some support, as does the scene where Reid asks questions of the entire Fasnacht family. When asked what was most memorable to him, Reid quickly recounts his interview with Al that took place with them both on Merry-Go-Round horses with the ride in motion.

"I still remember my favorite question, which was, 'When did you retire,

Al?' and he said, '25 years ago.' And I said, 'How many days do you work now?' And he said, 'Seven.' I said, 'Seven days a week; that's quite a retirement you've got there,'" Reid said. "At another point during the interview, he said that when he's not working during the summer he wishes he was. You can see what a wonderful man he is, and that has made its way down to the younger generations.

"When people ask me what my favorite story is, at one end of the spectrum I always say, being embedded with the Marines in Iraq for five or six weeks, because it was such an eye-opener for me. But on the other end, it is the people stories, and I always mention this story – stories that really hit you in the heart more than in the head – and this is that kind of story."

Rabin had a chance encounter with Al the following summer that reinforced her thoughts about him and what made him special while filming the story the summer before.

"I went back to Funland the next summer, as I always do, and we ran into Al. This was total coincidence; he didn't know we were coming, and I didn't know he would be there," Rabin said. "As I was getting out of my car he said, 'Hi Carrie,' and I was shocked that A, he remembered me and B, he knew my daughter's name."

Many factors go into determining what makes it on television. Rabin said Funland's affordability was a very important element in the story of an old-fashioned amusement park that caters to families.

"One of the things we were really struck by was the prices, and Al's determination to keep prices low so that families could afford it," Rabin said. "I don't know if we would have done the story if the family was charging $5 a ticket. It's very rare these days that you hear about people who could charge more charging less so that more families can get enjoyment."

Reid and Rabin had heard the stories about multiple generations of families who had all ridden the same Funland rides. The challenge

Three generations of the Penta family have enjoyed Funland.

would be to find one such family at the park soon after it opened that Friday. This "family testimonial" is a critical piece to the narrative; it adds a sense of authenticity and believability. It is one thing for the Fasnacht family to talk glowingly about Funland, and quite another for customers to do so. It did not take the CBS team long to find what it was looking for.

"We knew we wanted to find a family with several generations who had experienced Funland. We didn't realize it would be so easy," Rabin said. "Literally the first family we went up to, we said, 'Is this your first trip to Funland?' and the grandmother said, 'Oh no, I came when I was a kid, and I brought my children, and now they are bringing their children.' So we knew it held a lot of memories for families who have been coming for generations; we had no idea our story would spur so many people to pack up and go who had never heard of it."

◆ ◆ ◆ ◆

Not only does Funland create memories; it seems to foster the sharing of those memories to Fasnacht family members and others. In hearing many of those recollections myself from Funland customers over the years, I got the sense people were able to relive those happy moments this way, with Al and his family the beneficiaries.

"We still have many individuals that out of the blue will come up to any of us, and my sense is they feel they have to share their 'story' about what Funland has meant to them," said third-generation family member Randy Curry. "The responses and connections we make with the families that feel they need to share their story is evidence that we offer something special."

Both Rabin and Reid concur.

"It's old-fashioned values. It's keeping prices reasonable, it's real caring attention to the customers, it's being meticulously safe with the rides, it's not trying to do the latest thing that comes along but doing the things that they've been doing for years and doing them better and with more care than anyone else," Reid said. "And just having this safe, family environment is hard to find on a boardwalk. There's a lot of stuff on boardwalks where parents want to be there because they don't want their kids to be alone, but at Funland, you can just let the kids go. It's such a warm and safe place."

Adds Rabin: "It is like a blast from the past, or a look back in time. The rides are the same as they were 50 years ago, and the prices have been kept very low. I think for a lot of families with those memories that they have when they were there, and for new families discovering it, it still feels like a throwback, it still feels like a fun, safe, joyful experience that you can't find in many other places."

The show ends with Reid asking Al what the secret has been for his family to be able to work together for so many years. "Love," Al said. "Love is the secret."

Love indeed.

MY FUNLAND STORY: Stephanie Lemke

My son, Jonathan, was born on the Fourth of July, and I went to Rehoboth in August of 1991 for the first time with my sister and niece. On that trip we discovered Funland. We then started going to Rehoboth and Funland every year, and we haven't missed a year yet. We got to know the Fasnacht family just from going to Funland. They are wonderful people; I couldn't picture ever going to Rehoboth without spending time with them.

Jon also grew to be the best at the Goblet Toss, holding the record of winning 15 silvers in one week. Brad Ginder from the Fasnacht family presented him with a trophy – a silver-painted goblet with a Wiffle Ball.

Before we became really good friends with the Funland folks, my dad got in trouble because he would 'trick ride' on the Merry-Go-Round. And I think that is one of the things that broke the ice with them. They had to tell this gentleman to ride properly on the horse because he was spinning around and riding backwards and doing all of this crazy stuff.

During our annual trips, my mom [Margaret Shirley "Peggy" Thomas] and dad [Gottlieb "Fred" Thomas] would come in Funland and Al would see them, and they struck up a friendship that was just amazing. We always come to Funland the same week, and one year we changed the date and Brad called us and said, "Where are you? Aren't you supposed to be here today?"

My parents were celebrating their 60th wedding anniversary in 2016, and I wanted to surprise them with a renewal of their wedding vows. My first thought was to do it on the beach in Rehoboth. I asked Brad and Al if they would be dad's best men, and they said yes. I told them what would be really cool is to have the ceremony at the Merry-Go-Round in Funland, which was my dad's favorite ride. Brad said, "Why can't you? It would be perfect to do it there."

Peggy and Fred Thomas and family and friends after renewing their wedding vows at Funland.

So that's what we did, on July 8, 2016. It was a complete surprise. My parents didn't know until they came in and saw everyone. Then Neil [Fasnacht] gave my mom this big stuffed animal for a wedding gift that fit right in her go-cart basket. They are the greatest people. I know my dad was so excited when Al and Brad stood for him that day.

Last year, my dad passed away in Rehoboth exactly one year to the day after my parents renewed their vows at Funland. As soon as word spread around the beach, members of the Fasnacht family came running to see us. That's how close they were to my parents. They were like right there, offering to help us any way they could. They helped my family get through that day and on our way home to Maryland. They are the kind of people who would give you the shirt off their back if you needed it; very generous, loving people. We are proud to call the Fasnacht family our beach family!

CHAPTER 16:
The Future of Funland

"All of our generation want to keep Funland a successful
family-owned business far into the future. We are the guardians of the park
and the experience Al and my grandfather Don and their parents created.
There are challenges ahead, but we are determined to succeed."
– Ian Curry, fourth-generation family member

Funland in the 1970s.

The future of Funland is perhaps less clear now than it has ever been. To date, the second and third generations have done the heavy lifting, providing the ride maintenance, managing the books and personnel and doing whatever needs to be done, at any hour of the day or night, to keep the park running smoothly. The results speak for themselves. Funland has hundreds of thousands of visitors each year, many of whom come back every summer, for a variety of reasons: the park's welcoming, family-friendly and relaxed atmosphere; the low prices and the nostalgic and timeless feel; the multi-generational experience of going on the same rides and playing the same games; and the sense of safety, both personal and on the rides, that visitors often mention they feel in few other places outside of their homes. In short, it's about making memories.

The second generation, though, is now in their late 80s and early 90s, and the third generation range from their mid-50s to almost 70. While the third generation is not planning to step aside completely anytime soon, the torch is being passed to the fourth generation. Things at Funland have been done pretty much the same way since 1962 – family members are given jobs that they do to the best of their abilities, and they help others when their jobs are completed. There is also a set of unwritten rules all family members pretty much abide by:

- Set a good example for the hired summer employees, especially in doing undesirable tasks

- Provide great customer service and treat others as you'd like to be treated

- Focus on ride safety; warn customers about potential dangers, and stop a ride if anything seems amiss

- Hustle at all times. Doing so can shorten the long lines at rides and games and creates a sense of efficiency

Those rules will likely never change. Much, though, has changed in the almost 60 years the Fasnacht family has owned Funland. Consider the impact of just one new technology: cell phones. That is Funland employees' preferred way to communicate, to apply for a job, to check their work schedule, to inform their boss they can't come to work, and much more. And while employees are not allowed to use their phones while working, the personnel manager simply needs to be willing and able to communicate with employees via their phones.

◆ ◆ ◆ ◆

Speaking of personnel, that job may have changed more over the years than any other. When I worked at Funland in the 1980s, there were 26 full-time guys combined on the two shifts, plus lots of part-time workers. Now there are more than 125 summer workers. In my day, it was common for people to work four, five or six summers or more. That is not the case anymore. High school and college kids have many other interests competing for their time, so for many years, Funland has relied in part on kids from foreign countries to augment its workforce.

Those kids, though, are not likely to return for more than two or three summers, and many do just one. Another big change is that the park is open longer each day; the amusement games, redemption games (which award tickets rather than prizes) and the arcade all open at 10 am. You need workers to cover all those spots, which adds to the scheduling challenges, especially

Funland has had more summer employees from foreign countries, like this group from Lithuania.

with the Fasnacht family's desire to have people work different rides and games, even in the same day.

"We are having a hard time retaining people for multiple years," said personnel manager Chris Darr. "We may have 40 or 50 percent who come back for a second summer, and then we have a sharp drop off. There are so many things competing for people's time. Take sports. If you want to be on the best team, it's now a year-round thing. And a lot of the students say they can't come back for a third summer because they need to get an internship. I have full-time people starting as late as July, and I have full-time people leaving as early as the end of July. Whereas you used to have a full crew, that once they were trained were pretty much good to go all summer, now there is constant churn to the system. That's hard to manage, considering how much time and effort it takes to train staff and then the yearly turnover on top of that, it does make it harder for the workers to connect with each other.

"As we look to the future, we're constantly thinking, 'How do we adapt, how do we meet their needs from a technology perspective, such as creating a scheduling app that they can check on their phones, and how do we make working here as fun as possible?' The way to do that is to give them lots of different things to do, both at work – having them operate many different rides and games to get those experiences and to not get bored – and before and after work by organizing activities like sub night, pizza night, bumper car night and tournaments on games like Skee-Ball and Whac-a-Mole, where they can get to know one another. It makes for a long day, but we find the kids really enjoy these sort of events, and are still talking about them the next day."

Technology and hiring and staffing are just two of many areas changing the way businesses are run. The challenge for the younger generations of the Fasnacht family is how to preserve Funland's culture, tradition and values while adapting to present-day realities.

"We are aware at some point it is going to be our generation's responsibility to keep Funland going and keep it successful so that we can pass it on to our kids," said fourth-generation family member Mark Henschke. "The previous generations have set us up for success. One challenge with our generation is there are more roles to fill than we have people, so we may have to look outside for some skilled maintenance. We need to be careful not to get stretched too thin, but I think we are on the right path."

Adds fellow fourth-generation family member Erin Darr: "Our goal is to have Funland transition to our generation and to have nobody on the outside realize that. We don't want the heart of Funland to get lost as it gets passed down. I hope there isn't a lot of change and that Funland continues to stay the way it is, true to our image.

"Funland is like another family member. It's this living and breathing thing. When the doors go up at the start of the season it's exciting; when the doors come down at the end of the season it's bittersweet. Funland has shaped who I am; not just the business but also having my family around, and I want that to be around for my kids, and for their kids."

◆ ◆ ◆ ◆

The family is working with the Delaware Valley Family Business Center to help it with this generational transition.

"The third generation are not kids anymore, so we are doing a lot of talking with the next generation about taking over even more than they already have, and Delaware Valley is helping us with that," said Craig Fasnacht. "The fact that we are heading from the

Fourth-generation family member Ian Curry restocking a game.

third to the fourth generation, with the fifth generation on the distant horizon, is a neat thing, but it is also dangerous, because you want to keep everyone happy, but the nature of a family business is that you can't fire anybody, at least not easily. We've been very lucky so far that nobody is a lazy person or just wants to draw a paycheck."

One of the biggest changes for the family over the years is the workload, both during the season and in the off-season (mid-September through April). There was a time when none of the rides or games opened until 1 pm. For some time now, the games have opened at 10 am. And the sheer volume of customers, much greater now than it was in the 1980s when I worked at Funland, has an impact on all aspects of the business, from ride maintenance to closing time – and thus on the family itself.

"We work a lot of 16-hour days during the season, but I get a lot of satisfaction from seeing something that we take apart each year and put together and that brings so much joy to so many people," said Randy Curry. "As for the off-season, when I first started [in the late 1970s] there were months on end when I did not come down to Rehoboth. Come March, we'd be down here four or five days a week, but now we're working much more in the off-season."

All businesses face challenges, and Funland is no exception. The only amusement park in Delaware, though, also has a lot of factors in its favor. It has no competition; it has a great, boardwalk-facing location on property that is paid for; and it has a tradition and reputation for providing fun for the whole family at an affordable cost.

"There is always going to be a need for those smaller, lower-cost and less-crowded facilities for families to escape for a few hours," said amusement park historian Jim Futrell. "People don't always want to go to a big park; that is a big endeavor. A place like Funland, right there on the boardwalk, as long as the Atlantic Ocean is there, I think Funland is going to be just fine.

"One of the things you see in most successful family-owned parks is that the owners tend to be hands-on operators. They grow up in the business, they know the business, they know the customers, they are there to resolve issues quickly and make decisions quickly, so it makes them a little more adaptable to the marketplace. Funland's always had that very deeply involved ownership."

◆ ◆ ◆ ◆

In some ways, Rehoboth now relies on Funland, one of its most notable attractions, to continue bringing families with kids to this resort town about 20 miles north of Ocean City, Maryland. One of the main differentiators between Rehoboth and Ocean City is that Rehoboth has more of a family-friendly feel, and Funland is a big part of that.

Funland is Rehoboth's go-to place for family fun.

"The element of entertainment, happiness and joy that is lent to Rehoboth by Funland, especially for families with kids, is irreplaceable," said former Rehoboth Mayor John Hughes. "It is an anchor business. It is the fulcrum on which the whole business community pivots and operates. If they sold it for high-rises or apartments, it would change the nature of Rehoboth. But it is unlikely they will ever pull out. They are the kind of people you don't worry about something like that. You know they are essentially forever."

One thing all family members share is the pride they feel in Funland and what it has meant to so many people for the last half-century and more. Regardless of generation or whether they work at the park full time or not, taking the risk to buy Sport Center in 1962 weeks after a 50-year storm and run two amusement parks in two states was a gamble. Deciding to focus on the Rehoboth park and turning it into a summer destination and tradition for families in Delaware, Washington D.C., Baltimore, Philadelphia and beyond is a legacy the family cherishes.

"We want to do a good job, we want to give a source of entertainment to people and we don't want to gouge them or try to be more than what we are," said Lee Ann Fasnacht. "We all want to work together. And part of it is pride. Hey, we can do this. We're doing something different, and something we enjoy. We want to succeed. We want to stay together. We want to keep going."

MY FUNLAND STORY: Beth and Davies Storrs

Three generations of the Storrs family, including Beth (third from the right) and Davies (second from the right), continue to enjoy Funland.

Davies: After Beth and I got married, I took her to Funland in 1979, and we decided when we had kids to start going there, too. We had three kids and we got to see them ride the same rides, and now we are doing the same with our two grandkids. So three generations riding the Boats and those little jet rides. The cool thing is those two rides are in the same place they were when I first visited in the late 1950s. When you walk in the right side of the park, they are right there. A lot of good memories.

Beth: Davies told me so much about Funland, and I went there thinking, "Nothing could match Myrtle Beach, because we went every single night to the park there when I was a kid." I was just floored with how special Funland was. We tried going back to Myrtle Beach once and it's just not the same thing. But you return to Funland and it takes you right back to where you were; it's like stepping back in time. You can't do that anywhere else but at Funland.

The best thing about Funland is that it has not changed. When you go on vacation, you don't want the glitz and glamour you're hit with every day from television and all that. You want that small-town feel, and the childlike quality, that we all need to be the perfect vacation spot, and that's what Funland does.

Davies: When people ask us where we go for vacation and we say, "Rehoboth Beach," they don't understand that because we live in Virginia Beach.

But Rehoboth Beach is a lot different. The boardwalk is a mile long, and as a parent you feel you can let your kids go and you don't have to worry about them. Plus, you park your car when you arrive and you walk everywhere during the week. Most importantly, though, Rehoboth Beach, and Funland, is where our kids wanted to go.

Beth: Since we live at the beach, the main draw of Rehoboth isn't the beach; it is the boardwalk and Funland. It's as much for the adult kids as it is for the grandkids. When we get down there, we all go play Whac-a-Mole, we go on some rides and we can let the kids do their thing and go sit on the boardwalk. There is something for everybody. It doesn't get any better.

One of our favorite rides is the Haunted Mansion. I remember taking my daughter and her friend on it when they were in high school. They thought this was cheesy or whatever. At one point during the ride, I was in the middle and both of them were practically in my lap because something jumped out from one side, and it scared all of us. It was a big deal when our kids were old enough to ride, and our grandkids, who are 4 and 7, aren't quite there yet.

Funland reminds me of that scene in the movie Field of Dreams, where James Earl Jones's character [Terence Mann] is trying to convince Kevin Costner's character [Ray Kinsella] to build the Field of Dreams. Jones says it is not about the prices, but the memories that will make the field a success over a long period of time. ["The memories will be so thick they'll have to brush them away from their faces. … This field, this game; it's a part of our past, Ray. It reminds us of all that once was good, and that could be again. Oh … people will come, Ray. People will most definitely come."]

Rehoboth without Funland? It would be just another beach. What would you do at night or on a rainy day?

Davies: I don't think there's any question that another three or four generations of our family will experience Funland.

Acknowledgments

When I approached Al Fasnacht with the idea of writing a book on Funland and his family in the summer of 2017, he said if it was something that meant a lot to me, he was willing to help. From that point on he was all in. He sat down for numerous interviews, pulled together photos, letters, historical information and lists of people to talk to, encouraged his family to help me and offered words of support throughout the process. He even called me every few weeks to see how the book was coming and what he could do to assist. Spending time with Al was the best part of writing this book. He is, simply, one of a kind. I hope my writing has done him justice.

The entire extended Funland family, made up of the Fasnacht, Henschke, Curry, Darr, Ginder, Hendricks and Golaszewski families, was incredibly helpful; I owe a debt of gratitude to them all. Don, Craig, Neil, Gail, Gwen, Lisa, Lee Ann, Amy, Bill, Randy, Barb, Cindy, Brad, Todd, Elisabeth, Steve, Ian, Mark, Chris, Erin, Fiona, Lynne, Nathan, Amy G, Lauren, Greg and everyone else, thank you. It's easy for me to see why you are a fourth-generation family business, with the fifth not far behind.

Many of the book's photos, including the cover shots, are from Gregg Patrick Boersma, a good friend and skilled photographer. Gregg's energy and commitment were evident on a 14-hour day of shooting at Funland, when he took more than 800 photos. He was willing to try anything to get the perfect shot, and he single-handedly got the cover photo at the very end of the marathon day at Funland through sheer determination. Thanks, Gregg, for believing in me and this project.

Thanks to the many former Funland employees willing to offer their memories, stories and photos. Ours is a shared experience, as we will forever be part of the Funland family. Your insight into that world and the life lessons you learned provide a unique, behind-the-scenes perspective this book is much better for.

To the many Funland customers I spoke with, thank you for your energy and passion, and for describing what makes the park special to you and your family. These interviews were always fun in that I never knew what people were going to say. They talked about the park having a smell of summer, fun and nostalgia; of generations of families riding the same ride; of low prices and family fun; and of how they had smiles on their faces just talking about Funland.

Many friends and others contributed in ways big and small, and I thank you all: Todd Baldwin, Michelle Bamburak, Jewell Benford, Alexandra Bessent,

Sharon Boston, Kim Davidson, Bill Doney, Keith Donohue, Barbara Esstman, Mitch Gerber, Neal Gillen, Anne Haddad, Chris Hart, Kathy Herceg, Andrew Kleine, Karen Lancaster, Chris Lewkovich, Chris Raymond, Mike Ruddock, Michael Schwartzberg, Colin Stevens, Laurie Strongin, Mike Tidabock and Karen Warmkessel.

Finally, to my family. My dad got to know Al on our summer vacations to Rehoboth that started when I was 4, which led to my working at Funland. Dad told everyone he could how great a job it was, and he was right. My mom has always been my biggest supporter. From the time I first mentioned this project, she was convinced I would complete it, even when I wasn't. She would find the good in every chapter and share that with me. Thanks, mom, for being the dream book critic.

My wife Deborah has been very understanding about my "book time," and my devoting large chunks of several family vacations to this endeavor. Son Graham convinced me that self publishing was the way to go, and I enjoyed spending time with daughter Olivia at Funland as she filmed several pieces for the book website. I'm lucky to have had so many supportive people in my corner, and I thank everyone with a connection to this book.

About the Author

Chris Lindsley has 35 years of writing and editing experience, mostly in sports and health care. His six summers operating rides and games as part of the Funland family in the early 1980s taught him more about life, hard work and customer service than any job he's had before or since. He lives in Takoma Park, Maryland, with his wife and two children.

www.Land-of-Fun.com